2nd Edition

AP® COMPUTER SCIENCE PRINCIPLES CRASH COURSE®

By Jacqueline Corricelli, M.S.

Research & Education Association
www.rea.com

Research & Education Association
258 Prospect Plains Road
Cranbury, New Jersey 08512
Email: info@rea.com

AP® COMPUTER SCIENCE PRINCIPLES CRASH COURSE,® 2nd EDITION

Published 2022
Copyright © 2021 by Research & Education Association.
Prior edition copyright © 2018 by Research & Education Association.
All rights reserved. No part of this book may be reproduced in any
form without permission of the publisher.

Printed in the United States of America

Library of Congress Control Number 2021901681

ISBN-13: 978-07386-1265-2
ISBN-10: 0-7386-1265-0

AP® Computer Science Principles Crash Course
TABLE OF CONTENTS

ABOUT OUR BOOK

REA's *AP® Computer Science Principles Crash Course, 2nd Edition* is designed for the last-minute studier or any student who wants a quick refresher on the AP® course. The *Crash Course* is based on the latest *AP® Computer Science Principles Course and Exam Description* and focuses only on the topics tested, so you can make the most of your study time.

Written by an award-winning AP® Computer Science Principles test expert, our *Crash Course* gives you a concise review of the major concepts and important topics tested on the AP® Computer Science Principles exam.

- **Part I** explains the intricacies of the **Create Performance Task**, including how to produce your video and journal your development processes.

- **Part II** tackles the **End-of-Course Exam**, explaining the key topics found on the exam and strategies for successfully completing the exam. You'll also find AP®-style practice questions to prepare you for what you'll see on test day.

- Handy **appendices** include a glossary of computer terms you need to know, as well as helpful links and the exam reference sheet.

- **Sneak Peek:** These examples are similar to questions you might see on your AP® Computer Science Principles Exam.

ABOUT OUR ONLINE PRACTICE EXAM

How ready are you for the *AP® Computer Science Principles* exam? Find out by taking REA's online practice exam available at *www.rea.com/studycenter*. This test features automatic scoring, detailed explanations of all answers, and diagnostic score reporting that will help you identify your strengths and weaknesses so you'll be ready on exam day.

Whether you use this book throughout the school year or as a refresher in the final weeks before the exam, REA's *Crash Course* will show you how to study efficiently and strategically, so you can boost your score.

Good luck on your AP® Computer Science Principles exam!

ABOUT OUR AUTHOR

Jacqueline "Jackie" Corricelli teaches AP® Computer Science Principles at Conard High School, West Hartford, Connecticut. A public school educator since 2003, Corricelli was a Phase II Pilot Instructor for AP® CS Principles. She has been a table leader for the AP® CS Principles Reading since the first reading in 2017 and she also works as an AP® CS Principles Reading consultant.

In 2020, Corricelli was named to the inaugural cohort of the Computer Science Teachers Association Equity Fellowship. In 2017, she was one of 10 teachers honored with the Computer Science Teaching Excellence Award, sponsored by InfoSys Foundation USA; the Association for Computing Machinery, the world's leading computing society; and the Computer Science Teachers Association. Corricelli is also a 2013 recipient of the Presidential Award for Excellence in Mathematics and Science Teaching, the highest honor bestowed by the United States government for K–12 mathematics and science (including computer science) teaching.

The author, a former radar systems engineer, is a member of the Connecticut State Department of Education CS Advisory Group, created to improve access to and define computer science education at the state level. She also serves as President of the Connecticut Computer Science Teachers Association and is a CS for ALL SCRIPT Facilitator.

Corricelli earned a B.A. in mathematics and statistics from the University of Connecticut and an M.S. in mathematics secondary education at Westfield State University in Massachusetts. She is a certified mathematics and computer science teacher. She and her family reside in East Granby, Connecticut.

She dedicates this book to her daughter, Genevieve.

ABOUT REA

Founded in 1959, Research & Education Association (REA) is dedicated to publishing the finest and most effective educational materials—including study guides and test preps—for students of all ages.

Today, REA's wide-ranging catalog is a leading resource for students, teachers, and other professionals. Visit *www.rea.com* to see a complete listing of all our titles.

ACKNOWLEDGMENTS

We would like to thank Pam Weston, Publisher, for setting the quality standards for production integrity and managing the publication to completion; Heidi Gagnon, Digital Content Specialist, for coordinating the development of the REA Study Center; Larry B. Kling, Editorial Director, for overall direction; Fiona Hallowell, Editor, for editorial project management; Kathy Caratozzolo of Caragraphics for typesetting this edition; and Jennifer Calhoun for file prep.

We would also like to extend our appreciation to Robert Juranitch, M.S. Ed., for his technical edit of the manuscript. Mr. Juranitch currently teaches AP® Computer Science Principles at The University School of Milwaukee, Milwaukee, Wisconsin.

Keys for Success
on the AP® Computer
Science Principles Exam

The AP® Computer Science Principles course and exam can be completed successfully by anyone who has access to a computer and a love of learning. In your research about this AP® course and exam, you have probably noticed that there are quite a few different ways to learn what you need to know. You might have explored some websites and realized that you need a way to (1) get the essential knowledge, (2) figure out what you need to do to score well, and (3) find one resource (rather than twenty different tabs) that you can trust.

This *Crash Course* is here to help you get the best score on your AP® exam by providing the information that you need to know, a plan for how to manage your time to complete the performance task, and resources that you can trust.

Remember: Succeeding on the AP® Computer Science Principles exam is definitely within your reach, especially when you study strategically with this *Crash Course* book!

KEY 1: UNDERSTAND THE STRUCTURE OF THE EXAM

This exam consists of two parts: a performance task and an End-of-Course multiple-choice exam. Student performance is measured on a 5-point scale. Thirty percent of your score comes from the performance task and 70% of your score comes from the End-of-Course Exam. The performance task is completed and submitted to the College Board prior to taking the End-of-Course Exam, which is administered in May.

- **The Create Performance Task**

    This task is worth 30% of your AP® exam score and takes a minimum of 12 hours to complete. The task involves creating a program as a way to express yourself, solving a problem, or better understanding something.

You will need to have access to a computer to type your responses and to create your program.

In this task, you will design a program of your choice and you will submit the program code and a video of your program running. You will also submit written responses about your program to prompts provided by the College Board. Part I of this book focuses on helping you with the Create Performance Task.

- **The End-of-Course Exam**

The final part of the AP® Computer Science Principles course is the End-of-Course Exam. This is a multiple-choice exam that contains 70 questions with four answer choices: (A) through (D). It is worth 70% of your AP® score, and 2 hours is allotted to complete the exam.

KEY 2: UNDERSTAND HOW THE EXAM IS SCORED AND WHAT IT MEANS

Your Create Performance Task and your End-of-Course Exam will be scored independently.

The End-of-Course Exam is scored by machine. There are three types of questions and there is no partial credit for any of these question types.

(1) Single-Select Multiple-Choice—only one answer choice is correct

(2) Reading Passage Multiple-Choice—one reading passage is used for five single-select questions

(3) Multiple-Select Multiple-Choice—two answer choices are correct

Each of the 70 questions is worth one point and your score is based on the number of questions answered correctly. Points are not deducted for incorrect answers and no points are awarded for unanswered questions, so it is in your best interest to answer every question. For the multiple-select multiple-choice questions, you must choose *both* of the correct answers to receive credit.

The Create Performance Task is scored during the annual AP® Reading, which takes place in June. AP® Computer Science Principles and college instructors apply scoring guidelines, which are publicly available, and award points based on these guidelines. There are six different categories used to score the Create Performance Task. Each of these categories are worth 5 points. There is no partial credit for each category. The Create Performance Task is worth 30 points in total.

The 70 points from the End-of-Course Exam and 30 points from the Create Performance Task are then combined and converted to a 1-to-5 AP® scale.

The College Board ranks your combined score in one of five categories to indicate your college readiness:

    5—extremely well qualified

    4—well qualified

    3—qualified

    2—possibly qualified

    1—no recommendation

An AP® grade of 3 or more means that a student has shown mastery of course content that would be covered in an introductory computer science course intended for non-STEM majors.

Some colleges and universities accept scores of 3, 4, or 5 for college credit, while others only accept 4s and 5s. Some colleges do not award credit for an AP® test. It is important that you research the policies of the colleges you are interested in attending. Also, be aware that colleges and universities can change their AP® acceptance policies at any time. Check with the college you are interested in to see what score is required to receive credit or to see if it fills a prerequisite for another course. To see policies for AP® scores by school, the College Board has created this link: *apstudents.collegeboard.org/getting-credit-placement/search-policies.*

Test Tip *Even if a college does not award placement credit for an AP® exam, taking an AP® test may strengthen your college application because you rose to the "AP® challenge."*

KEY 3: BUDGET TIME TO COMPLETE THE CREATE PERFORMANCE TASK

There are no surprises with the Create Performance Task since the task itself and the scoring guidelines are both available online. You will need to complete this task before May. You can find the task and the guidelines here at any time: *apstudents. collegeboard.org/courses/ap-computer-science-principles*.

If you already know a programming language, twelve hours to complete the task is a reasonable estimate. If you do not know a language, more time will be required.

This *Crash Course* will support you with planning and programming strategies. Efforts planning your approach, designing your code, and revising your code and written responses will be time well spent.

Part I of this book focuses on helping you complete this task.

KEY 4: UNDERSTAND THE CONTENT TESTED ON THE END-OF-COURSE EXAM

The topics covered on the End-of-Course Exam are as follows:

Concept (Big Idea)	Percentage of Multiple-Choice Questions that will be about this Big Idea	Approximate Number of Multiple-Choice Questions (out of 70) that will be about this Big Idea
Algorithms and Programming	30%–35%	21–25 questions
Impact of Computing	21%–26%	15–18 questions
Data	17%–22%	12–15 questions
Computer Systems & Networks	11%–15%	8–11 questions
Creative Development	10%–13%	7–9 questions

Part II of this book focuses on helping you get ready for these questions and concludes with 25 sample multiple-choice questions.

KEY 5: UNDERSTAND THE COLLEGE BOARD'S DIGITAL PORTFOLIO

You will be using the College Board's Digital Portfolio, a web-based application, to submit the Create Performance Task. You will submit your video, program code, and your responses to the writing prompts to this application to complete this task.

Your AP® teacher will receive approval at the start of the school year to access the Digital Portfolio. Any teacher who has passed the AP® Course Audit process will be able to log in to the Digital Portfolio as a teacher. This is true even if the course is being completed via an online platform or if a home-schooling parent passes the course audit. The teacher will set up a class that you will need to access. If you have taken an SAT® or PSAT,® you most likely already have an account with the College Board. You will use the same login information to go to *collegeboard.org/ digital-portfolio* and connect your account to your AP® Computer Science Principles class. Your AP® teacher will confirm your enrollment.

Once done, you'll be all set to submit your Create Performance Task and indicate your intent to take the End-of-Course Exam.

Remember, your final performance task program code, video, and written responses must be submitted by the end of April.

KEY 6: SUPPLEMENT YOUR *CRASH COURSE*

REA's *Crash Course* contains *essential* information for the AP® Computer Science Principles tasks and End-of-Course Exam. You should, however, supplement this book with materials from your course and the College Board.

The *AP® Computer Science Principles Course and Exam Description* booklet from the College Board shares information about the course and the exam, including sample questions. Additionally, the College Board's AP® Students website (*apstudents. collegeboard.org/courses/ap-computer-science-principles*) contains review materials, including sample responses for the performance task and scoring guidelines.

KEY 7: HANDLING EXAM DAY

1. Plan to show up at the exam site at least 20 minutes before the scheduled start time for the exam.

2. Bring two fresh No. 2 pencils with clean erasers and a government issued or school issued photo ID.

3. Be prepared to turn in your cell phone and other electronic devices at the beginning of the exam. You might want to just leave them at home!

4. The exam proctor will read a lot of instructions—be patient. Plan to spend more than the allotted 2 hours at the exam site.

5. Answer every multiple-choice question, even if you have to guess. Remember, there is no deduction for an incorrect answer but no points can be earned for unanswered questions. If you're stuck, give it your best guess.

6. When you're done, relax . . . sit back and wait for your qualifying score to arrive!

Deciding on a Programming Language

I. REQUIREMENTS FOR THE PROGRAMMING LANGUAGE

A. You can study AP® Computer Science Principles using any language(s) you choose, provided it allows you to do all of the following:

1. evaluate expressions

2. develop procedures (or methods or functions) with parameters

3. use variables, lists (or any other collection such as an array), conditionals, and loops

B. This decision is important because it is likely that the language, or combination of languages, you choose will not only impact how you complete the Create Performance Task, but also how you prepare for many of the End-of-Course Exam questions.

II. DECIDING ON A BLOCK-BASED OR TEXT-BASED LANGUAGE

A. The language you choose can be block-based or text-based. There are pros and cons to each.

B. Features of a Block-Based Language

1. A block-based language uses a drag-and-drop programming approach where lines of code act like puzzle pieces that you can move around on the screen to write code.

2. With block-based languages, syntax guesswork is largely removed. For example, you would not need to worry about spacing to show correct indents, colons or semi-colons, or parentheses.

3. Block-based languages are usually created to do jobs in a specific environment.

   i. This means that programmers may have less control over the way a computer allocates resources.

   ii. This means that the code may need that environment to run. If the environment is internet-based, you will need internet access.

   iii. This means that you may be able to do some coding faster, without worrying about some of the details of implementation when you are coding in a block-based language.

   iv. Note that some block-based languages allow you to see the text version of block code.

C. Features of a Text-Based Language

   1. To use a text-based language, code is written using letters and characters on a keyboard.

   2. Syntax details in a text-based language would depend on the language.

   3. Text-based languages are often created to solve general problems in many environments.

      i. This means you may have more direct control over what the program is doing in terms of memory allocation and function creation when using a text-based language.

      ii. This means that you may be able to run your program in multiple environments even without internet access.

After you understand how expressions, loops, variable definitions, procedures, and lists work in the language you choose, the majority of your programming time should be spent planning, deciding the sequence and structures for your code, debugging, and testing. This is true no matter the programming language.

III. LANGUAGES TO CONSIDER

A. Here is a partial list of languages/applications that fit the needs of the Create Performance Task.

▸ Alice (*alice.org*)—allows you to create and animate 3D worlds; can use block-based approach or can use plug-in to code in java

▸ App Inventor (*appinventor.mit.edu*)—use a block-based language to create Android applications

▸ App Lab (*code.org/educate/applab*)—use this online environment to create apps that run in a device simulator; can toggle between text and block-based approach

▸ C languages (*docs.microsoft.com*)—this would include C, C++, and C#; these languages allow you to solve and model many problems. Choose your development environment carefully—some are purely online and some require a download.

▸ Greenfoot (*greenfoot.org*)—use java (text-based) to create 2D environments such as simulations or games

▸ Java (*java.com*)—created by Oracle; this text-based language allows you to solve and model many problems. You will want to choose your development environment carefully— some are purely online and some require a download.

▸ JavaScript—text-based language created by Oracle; you can use this language to create web-based applications and effects.

▸ Julia (*julialang.org*)—text-based language designed for scientific and numerical computing

▸ LEGO Mindstorms Ev3 (*education.lego.com*)—block-based language that allows you to use code to interact with a LEGO Mindstorm robot

▸ Microsoft Make Code (*microsoft.com/makecode*)—online environment that features several code interfaces allowing you to do things like interacting with hardware like micro:bit devices or creating arcade-like games; can toggle back and forth between text and block

▸ Processing (*processing.org*)—this text-based language allows you to create and interact with functions that generate objects like lines or shapes in a 2D plane.

▸ Python (*python.org*)—this text-based language allows you to solve and model many types of problems. You will want to choose your development environment carefully—some are purely online and some require a download.

▸ Quorum Programming Language (*quorumlanguage.com*)— originally designed for blind students, this environment contains many accommodations to make computer science more accessible to you

▸ R (*r-project.org*)—this text-based language was designed for data scientists to perform statistical analysis and create simulations.

▸ Ruby (*ruby-lang.org/edu*)—text-based language that features syntax that is similar to spoken-language

▸ Scratch (*scratch.mit.edu*)—this block-based online coding environment allows you to control sprites and their behaviors in an online 2D environment

- Snap! (*snap.berkeley.edu*)—this block-based online coding environment allows you to create your own blocks or use predefined blocks to control sprites and their behaviors in an online 2D environment

- Swift (*developer.apple.com/swift*)—text-based language that allows you to create iOS apps

- TI-Basic (*education.ti.com*)—this text-based language uses the TI graphing calculator development environment; can be used independently or in combination with the TI Innovator Hub.

B. Languages and Environments Change

1. Languages and environments are constantly evolving. Bear in mind that links may change over time.

2. You should use your favorite search engine to find up-to-date resources for the language that interests you the most.

3. There are many great tutorials online to allow you to experiment with these languages to help you with your decision.

Unless you are using a structured and planned curriculum, it may be better to spend time learning one language well rather than jumping around from language to language.

IV. **THE ROLE OF AN ENDORSED PROVIDER IN LANGUAGE CHOICE**

A. What are Endorsed Providers?

1. Endorsed Providers are groups of people who have carefully considered the requirements for the AP® CS Principles exam and Create Performance Task and have planned out material that teachers can use to support student learning.

2. The College Board endorses these providers because they not only meet the needs of the AP® CS Principles exam, but they are also able to provide sufficient access to curriculum and training for teachers.

3. Each provider is unique in approach and in sequencing of lessons.

4. Most providers do not offer direct online courses for students.

    i.   See part V (below) for providers that do offer online courses for students

    ii. To have access to the curricula listed here, your teacher would need to choose this course as their provider, get training, and then you would be able to take the course.

5. It is important that teachers research providers carefully.

    i.   Some providers charge a fee; others do not.

    ii. Some providers offer many locations for training, including virtual; others do not.

B. Endorsed Providers as of June 2020

Endorsed Provider	Language(s)/ Environment(s)	Link to Curriculum
Apple	Swift	*apple.co/apcsp*
Beauty and Joy of Computing (BJC)	Snap!	*bjc.edc.org*
CodeHS	JavaScript	*codehs.com*
Code.org	JavaScript, AppLab	*code.org/educate/ csp*
Code Train (for Canadian teachers only)	Processing, Java	*codetra.in*
CS Matters	Python	*curriculum. csmatters.org*

Endorsed Provider	Language(s)/ Environment(s)	Link to Curriculum
CS50	Scratch, C (in depth), JavaScript, Python, SQL	*cs50.harvard.edu/ ap/2020*
Edhesive	Scratch, Python	*edhesive. com/courses/ apcs_principles*
Mobile CSP	AppInventor	*mobile-csp.org/*
Project Lead the Way	Python	*pltw.org*
UTeach	Scratch, Python	*cs.uteach.utexas. edu*
Zulama by Carnegie Learning	GML	*emcp.com/ applied-learning/ zulama*

1. In addition to this list, teachers should be aware of AccessCSForAll. Based on the Code.org curriculum, AccessCSForAll is curriculum designed for teachers of neurodivergent learners. For more information about this curriculum, this link will help: *washington.edu/ accesscomputing/accesscsforall/get-involved/ap-computer-science-principles-professional-development-teachers-neurodivergent-learners*

2. Throughout the school year, it is possible that endorsed providers may be added to or removed from this list. The most up-to-date list of endorsed providers is available online here: *apcentral.collegeboard.org/courses/ ap-computer-science-principles/classroom-resources/ curricula-pedagogical-support*

V. ONLINE COURSES FOR AP® CS PRINCIPLES

A. What are Online Course Providers?

1. Online course providers are groups of people who have designed an AP® CS Principles class for students.

   i. They have received approval from the College Board because they are covering all required content.

   ii. This is a perfect option for you if you are taking this course on your own because your school does not offer the course yet or because you are home-schooled.

2. You can sign up directly with online course providers as a student.

B. List of Online Course Providers (as of June 2020)

Online Provider	Website	Student Eligibility
Edhesive	*edhesive.com/courses/apcs_principles*	Open to all students
Michigan Virtual	*michiganvirtual.org/students/high-school/advanced-placement*	Open only to Michigan students
North Carolina School of Science & Mathematics	*ncssm.edu*	Open only to North Carolina students
PVOnline High School	*pvschools.net/pvonline*	Open only to Arizona students
QSI Virtual School	*gold.qsi.org/qvs*	Open only to Quality Schools International students
Riverside Virtual School	*eoc.riversideunified.org/schools/riverside_virtual_school*	Open only to California students

Online Provider	Website	Student Eligibility
Scout from University of California	*ucscout.org*	Open to all students
SophieConnect	*sophieconnect.org*	Open to all students
Virtual High School	*vhslearning.org/*	Open to all students
Wisconsin Virtual School	*wisconsin.virtualschool. org*	Open to all students

Remember, it is possible that, over time, schools will be added to or removed from this list. Use this link to find the most recent updates to online course providers: *apstudents. collegeboard.org/courses/ap-computer-science-principles/ online-course-providers*

VI. YOUR GOAL WHEN LEARNING TO PROGRAM

A. You want to learn as much as you possibly can about the language you choose. The only way to do this is to program, make mistakes, learn from those mistakes, and try again.

B. Before attempting the Create Performance Task, you should be familiar enough with the language that you can do *all* of the following:

1. Define a list that will play an important role in fulfilling the goal of your program.

   i. For this key list (or any collection type), you need to:

      ▸ explain the data stored in the list.

      ▸ explain how the list manages complexity in the program.

      ▸ identify where in the code the list is being used.

2. Define a procedure that plays an important role in accomplishing the purpose of your program.

    i.   For this key procedure, you need to:

- ▸ be sure it has at least one parameter.
- ▸ define the data type of the input(s) to the procedure.
- ▸ define the data type of the output(s) from the procedure.
- ▸ explain why sequence (order) matters in the procedure.
- ▸ explain why selection (conditional statement(s)) matters in the procedure.
- ▸ explain why iteration matters in the procedure.
- ▸ explain how sequence, selection, and iteration execute in the program in detail.
- ▸ explain how you tested the procedure to be sure it worked with at least two different parameters.

C. Before attempting the End-of-Course Exam, you should be familiar enough with the language that you can do *all* of the following sample problems:

1. Accept a list (or collection) of integers as a parameter and find all of the following values using this list:

    i.   minimum

    ii. maximum

    iii. average

2. Generate a random number from 1 to the length of a list and return a random element stored in that list.

3. Accept a string as a parameter and do the following with the string:

   i. concatenate (attach) the string input to the procedure to another string

   ii. print the string concatenated to another variable

4. Return or print a value from a procedure.

5. Add or remove items to a list if something is true about them.

6. Count the number of times something happens.

7. Accept a number and a list as an argument and count the amount of times that number is found in the list.

8. Swap values stored in two different variables.

Test Tip

Time spent chasing errors and understanding how your chosen language works will be time well spent to maximize your score for both the Create Task and the End-of-Course Exam.

PART I

THE CREATE PERFORMANCE TASK

Planning Your Program

I. **OVERVIEW**

A. The Create Performance Task is about creating a program as a way to express yourself, solve a problem, or better understand something. It is worth 30% of your AP® Computer Science Principles score and it is due by April 30. The performance task consists of the following three parts:

1. Designing and creating the program

2. Debugging and testing the program

3. Documenting the program

B. When you finish the Create Performance Task, you will follow directions to submit the following items to the College Board via the Digital Portfolio:

1. Your entire program code.

2. A video of your program running as you described in the written response.

3. Your responses to written Prompts 3a through 3d.

C. The Create Performance Task should take about 12 hours to complete.

1. If you work 45 minutes per day on this task, it should take you about 15–16 days to finish. However, if you decide to use a programming language you do not know, the task could take significantly longer.

2. Assume that the overall plan for the task will look something like this:

Task Step	Approximate Time
Planning & Design	1 hour
Initial Code	1 hour
Revising & Testing Code	4 hours
Prepare Code for Final Submission	1 hour
Creating Video for Final Submission	1 hour
Written Response	4 hours

II. ABOUT THE CREATE PERFORMANCE TASK

A. The Create Performance Task is your chance to use a programming language to create something new.

B. The coding piece of the Create Performance Task can be done collaboratively, but you need to create your own video and your own written responses based on your unique contribution to the code.

C. Be sure to read the Create Performance Task prompts (Appendix C) and Create Performance Task Scoring Checklist (Appendix D). The checklist was created directly from the 2020–21 Scoring Guidelines. You can find these online here: *apstudents.collegeboard.org.* Click "Exam Page" to navigate to the guidelines and prompts.

D. To maximize your score, be sure to respond to each prompt clearly, and always cite any source to which you refer.

E. There are three parts to this performance task:

1. Designing your program

2. Coding your program

3. Documenting your program

III. HOW THE CREATE PERFORMANCE TASK RELATES TO THE SOFTWARE DEVELOPMENT CYCLE

1. The Software Development Cycle has four steps. You will go through each part of this cycle to complete this performance task. (We will discuss the first two steps of the Software Development Cycle in this chapter and the final two steps in Chapter 4.)

Step 1: IDEA

Define your vision for your program.
- Will you solve a problem?
- Will you learn something new?
- Will you create something with your program?
- Will you replicate a behavior?
- Will you generate a tool for others to use?

Step 2: DESIGN

Decide on the approach you will use for your program. Flowcharts, pseudocode, or some other visual mapping of your plan is common in this step.

Step 3: IMPLEMENT

Write your program based on your design.

Step 4: TEST

Fix what is not working to align your program with your idea.

IV. STEP 1 IN THE SOFTWARE DEVELOPMENT CYCLE—DEFINE YOUR VISION

A. Brainstorm about an idea for your program.

    1. Your program is the center of your Create Performance Task. Your program *must*:

        i. accept input from one or more of the following:

            ▸ user (including user actions that cause events to occur)

            ▸ a device

            ▸ an online data stream

            ▸ a file

        ii. use at least one list (or any other collection type) to represent a group of data that is being stored and used in your program.

            ▸ Besides lists, other examples of collection types are: arrays, databases, hash tables, dictionaries, and sets.

            ▸ The list should manage the complexity of your program. This means that the list:

                – is used to keep your code organized and readable

                – is named to represent a collection which is used at least once in your program

            ▸ This list should be there for one of two reasons:

                – it is necessary for your program

                – without it, your program would work differently

            ▸ This list should help fulfill the program purpose

                – have at least one procedure that does all of the following:

                    a. contributes to the program's intended purpose

    b. has one or more parameters (these are the variables that the procedure can receive as inputs)

– includes all of the following in its body:

    a. sequence: the order of the lines of code matter

    b. selection: there is a conditional (if/else if) statement that controls what the code does

    c. iteration: there is a loop

– the procedure is called by another part of the program

– the procedure produces an output (motion, sound, image, or text) and this output is related to both of the following:

    a. input to the procedure

    b. what the program is supposed to do

Test Tip

This may seem like a lot—and it is! It is crucial that you have done a lot of programming practice before you start your Create Performance Task. If you have not, or if you are learning a new language for the task, budget an extra 6–12 hours for this task in addition to the 12-hour requirement.

2. You need to be comfortable enough working in the programming language you choose that you can explain the following decisions you make about your program:

    i. The purpose of the program

    ii. How the program functions

    iii. The input and output of the program

    iv. The name of the key list, the data stored in the list, why this list is connected to your program's purpose, and how the list is helping you write better code

   v.   The name of the key procedure, why this procedure is connected to your program's purpose, and describe the key steps, the inputs/outputs, and key decisions being made by the procedure

  vi. How you tested the procedure to be sure it worked for multiple arguments to the procedure. When you explain this, you will need to:

> ▸ choose two calls to your procedure.

> ▸ explain how each of the two calls is testing a different section or condition in your code.

Test Tip

Do not worry yet about how you will do all of this explaining. Chapters 7–10 are designed to help you satisfy the writing requirements. Your priority now is deciding on your vision and your plan based on these known requirements.

3. When thinking about what program to write, focus on creating a program that means something to you.

4. Here are some questions to ask yourself to help generate ideas:

    i.   What programming language do I know well?

   ii. What behavior would I like to create in my program?

  iii. What game would I like to simulate?

  iv. What is the purpose I would like my program to fulfill?

   v. What problem would I like to solve with my program?

  vi. What could I build with my programming skill?

5. Decide if your brainstormed idea will put you in a good position to answer written responses. Your responses will be your opportunity to explain:

    i.   The purpose of your program

ii. The functionality of your program including:

  ▸ An important list (or any other collection type)

  ▸ Inputs and outputs

  ▸ A strong procedure you created, why you created it, and how it works

  ▸ The data used by your program

  ▸ How you know this functionality works (testing you completed)

  ▸ How this functionality helps you to accomplish the purpose of the program

Test Tip

The majority of the credit earned for the Create Performance Task comes from your ability to explain the decisions you made while coding.

6. You will know you have a good idea for your program if you can answer "yes" to each of the following questions:

Question	Yes	No
Is your idea interesting to you?		
Can you see how your idea can be accomplished using a language that you know well?		
Is your idea complex enough that it requires that data is stored as a list? (The list must be a useful or necessary addition to your code.)		
Is your idea complex enough that you will need a key procedure? (You will need to explain this procedure well. The procedure must require sequence, selection, and iteration and it must be connected to the program's purpose.)		
Is your idea complex enough that this key procedure will have at least one parameter? (You will need to explain the procedure in terms of inputs and outputs and how you tested that this parameter does what you said it does.)		

Take some time to check out the Create Performance Task samples that are on AP® Central. The College Board has collected samples of work completed by students just like you and provided their score and feedback to help you understand how the task and rubric will be used together to determine your grade. Go to apcentral.collegeboard.org.

B. Design Your Solution

1. Now that you have decided on a programming language and brainstormed about an idea, it is time to decide how to manage this idea and design your solution. We'll now explore Step 2 of the Software Development Cycle, Design. In this step, you will decide on the approach you want to use for your program. Flowcharts, pseudocode, or another visual mapping of your plan are common in this step.

2. Here are the likely decisions and recommended steps to designing a great solution.

   i. One of your first decisions is: Will I do this project independently or in collaboration with another programmer? There are benefits (and drawbacks) to each approach.

   ii. Consider the following points if you think you would like to work with someone else:

   ▸ Benefits

   – You will have help while brainstorming, coding, and debugging.

   – You will hear another person's ideas and see another person's approach.

   – You will make something larger than is needed for the Create Task.

▸ To make success likely, you will need to do a lot of planning and design ahead of coding.

– Both you and your partner will need to create your own video and your own written responses about the code. Only the code can be the same.

– This means that *each of you* will need to satisfy the list and procedure requirements with the code.

– To improve your chances for a successful partnership, you and your partner should:

    a. agree on the programming language.

    b. have significant experience using that programming language.

    c. understand that you will need to communicate regularly during each phase of the project.

▸ Begin thinking and deciding about how to divide the work. Here are some ideas for how to manage this:

– Approach 1: You and your partner plan your code. You decide the key list and key procedure you will use. You code your solution together. Note that the remainder of the project (the video and the written response) must be completed independently.

– Approach 2: You and your partner start your project together. You do not complete any of the required code with your partner. You work independently to complete the key list and the key procedure. Your partner does the same. You continue on to complete the video and written response independently.

a. You may need to meet many times per week to accomplish this task. This could be done with videoconferencing as long as you are both comfortable with using this tool.

b. You need to agree on how to share code ahead of time. Dropbox, Google Drive, or GitHub are commonly used if face-to-face work is inconvenient or not possible.

Test Tip

One way you can collaborate without coding together is to test the front-facing application. Your partner can suggest improvements without influencing your code. You would then decide if and how to implement this change.

iii. Consider the following points if you think you would like to do this task independently:

▶ Benefits:

 – You do not need to meet with someone else on a regular basis.

 – You can focus on your idea and if you need to change that idea, you would only impact yourself.

 – While planning, you would only need to include one key list and one key procedure that meets the project requirements.

 – If you learn well independently, you can spend more time learning about how to improve your project.

 – Since you wrote all of the code, completing the written response and video from your perspective will be easier.

iv. To make success likely, whether you are planning to work with someone or not, you should do all of the following:

> ▸ Have a plan (and a backup plan). Develop weekly goals. Include the amount of time you will spend on the project and what you hope to accomplish.

> ▸ Take frequent breaks. It is often better to work 1–2 hours, do something else, and then return to your project.

> ▸ Use concrete tools to manage your design. Suggestions are in Chapter 4.

V. TIPS FOR DESIGN

A. At a minimum, your design should answer the following questions:

1. Where does your program start and end?

2. Where will key decisions be made?

3. Which decisions need to happen in order and what is that order?

4. What is the input needed at key steps?

5. What is the output you expect at key steps?

6. Is there any repeated behavior? (That might make a great procedure!)

7. What is the key list that you will use in your program? (Remember—it needs to be helpful or necessary to accomplish the purpose.)

8. What data is stored in this list?

9. What is the key procedure you will use in your program? (Remember—it needs to (1) have sequence, selection, and iteration, (2) have at least one parameter, (3) be something that you can explain well.)

10. How will you know your procedure works for more than one type of input? (Remember—you will need to show how you tested the procedure to be sure that it worked for more than one condition.)

11. How will you manage your time?

12. What are some resources you might need to set up ahead of time so you can easily access them?

VI. TOOLS FOR DESIGNING

A. There are many tools that will help you design your program. Choose the tool that best meets your needs.

1. Write words as pseudocode.

   i. Pseudocode is a way to think through logic without worrying as much about the diagramming.

   ii. Look at pseudocode as logical steps that almost look like code, but are written in the language that you speak instead of one the computer understands.

2. Flowchart

   i. It is probably easiest to start on paper or using a whiteboard and markers.

   ii. You could also use computer-based tools like *draw.io* to create a flowchart.

   iii. Flowcharts are great for tracking the overall flow of your program and for planning out more complicated procedures.

iv. Start practicing with the symbols below. You will see them on your End-of-Course Exam.

Symbol	Meaning
OVAL	Indicates the beginning or end of a program.
ARROW	Shows relationships between parts of code; represents flow of information and/or logical path of code.
RECTANGLE	Indicates key step in logic that has one input and one output.
RHOMBUS	Shows a key decision; may be more than one input. Output will be Boolean (which can only be true or false).

3. Start trying ideas out in a coding "sandbox."

   i. A "sandbox" is an expression for a small area of code where you can play with your coding ideas without influencing the rest of the working program.

   ii. You could do this by commenting out code that works or by creating a new programming area where you can just focus on this one problem that requires extra attention.

   iii. Use extra output (more than what you would want in the program) or a debugger (if available in your language), to see more of what is happening at each step in the program.

   iv. Hybrid Approaches: Some people use all three tools. Others use Tool 1 and then go right to programming. Others jump right to Tool 3 or even make the change directly in their program. The approach you use depends on your comfort with the algorithm, the language, and your experience with programming.

v. Example: Finding the maximum of a list:

Suppose you wanted to create a procedure that takes a list as a parameter and returns the maximum value stored in that list.

▸ Using Tool 1:

–   You might start this work by planning the algorithm in words on paper.

–   You could figure out the algorithm by using something physical like 5 small pieces of paper. Write random numbers on one side (like {50, 90, 30, 70, 30}) and index numbers on the back. For 5 cards, the index numbers would be {1, 2, 3, 4, 5} or {0, 1, 2, 3, 4} depending on the language.

–   Note: Because the Exam Reference for the End-of-Course Exam numbers indices starting at 1, we will do that here.

In words, the algorithm might look something like this:

STEP 1: Get a list. Call it theList.

STEP 2: Initialize i to 1 and max to first element in theList.

STEP 3: Increment i.

STEP 4: If the next element in the list is larger than max, set max to the next element.

STEP 5: Repeat steps 3–4 until you reach the end of theList.

STEP 6: Return max.

▸ Using Tool 2:

As a flowchart, the algorithm might look something like the diagram that follows.

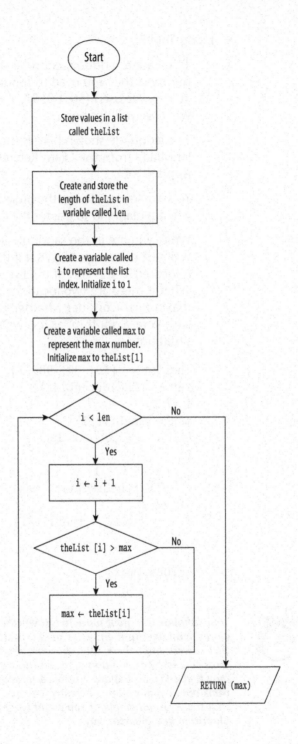

▸ Using Tool 3:

  – To create a sandbox, consider using the same
    numbers that you used to model the problem
    at first. We used {50, 60, 90, 70, 30}, so that is
    what we will use here.

  – The language shown here is the text-based
    language from the Exam Reference (see
    Appendix E).

  – You would want to use the programming language
    you are planning to use for the Create Task.

  – While you are in the sandbox, you might as
    well test other inputs. What if the maximum
    is located at the end of the list or at the start?
    What if there are two locations that hold the
    maximum? Consider whether you are happy
    with your algorithm, as it is written, for all
    situations.

```
theList ← [50, 60, 90, 70, 30]
len ← LENGTH(theList)
i ← 1
max ← theList[1]
REPEAT UNTIL (i ≥ len)
{
    i ← i + 1
    IF (theList[i] > max)
    {
        max ← theList[i]
    }
}
RETURN (max)
```

Test Tip

*Your sandbox is a great place to test whether your algorithm
works in all the situations you would expect. For example, if
theList were empty here, this algorithm would have a syntax
error caused by attempting to access theList[1] in this line:
max theList[1]. Seeing this possible error may force you to
think about your design differently; you may want to be sure
that theList is not empty or you might want to handle this
algorithm in a different way.*

VII. MAINTAINING YOUR DESIGN

A. Whether you decide to flowchart on paper or use one of the computer-based tools, you should do the following:

1. Keep your design close at hand and modify it frequently to be sure you are thinking about how any one change may influence the entire program.

2. Use this documentation to communicate with your partner, if you chose to work with another person. Use this documentation to help you remember key decisions you made if you are working independently.

VIII. JOURNALING

A. What is a Journal?

1. A journal (also called a written log) is a way to keep track of what you were thinking when you made key decisions while creating a program.

2. Journaling will help you reflect on how/why you made key decisions. Through this reflection you will grow as a programmer.

3. Journaling also helps you to maintain a schedule and catch areas that might require more time.

Test Tip

You should keep an independent journal even if you are working with someone else.

B. Setting up your Journal

1. Create a document (paper- or computer-based) with dates set up for each day that you plan to code. A table with the following column headers would work well:

Date	What did you accomplish today?	What do you need to do next?

2. Write each journal entry from your own perspective.

3. Remember your goals—you need a key procedure and you need a key list. The procedure needs to take at least one parameter and it must be crucial for the behavior of your whole program. The list must be necessary and it should help make something easier to accomplish in your program. These things should be built into your design.

4. When you add your key list, note:

   i.   how this list helps you accomplish your program's purpose

   ii. the data being stored in the list

   iii. where in the code the list is being used

   iv. why it is important or necessary for your program

5. When you add your key procedure, be sure to note each of the following details:

   i.   how this procedure helps you accomplish your program's purpose

   ii. how/where in the code the procedure is called

   iii. the input(s) and their data type

   iv. the output(s) and data type, if applicable

   v.   where sequence (order) of code matters in the procedure

   vi. where selection (conditional statements) matters in the procedure

vii. where iteration (looping) happened in the procedure

viii. how you tested the procedure to be sure:

▸ it worked for at least two different code segments

▸ the parameter you chose is connected to the functionality of the program

If you are reading this bulleted list and you are sure your design does not meet these needs, STOP now. Go back to the Design Phase and redesign. Alternatively, you may prefer to rethink your idea by broadening it and then redesigning. Do not worry. This is a totally normal part of process.

Now that you have an idea, a design, and an approach for how to document changes and key decisions, you are ready to program your Create Performance Task.

Creating Your Program

I. **OVERVIEW**

A. At this point you should have completed the following actions in your Create Performance Task:

1. You have decided on a programming language. (See Chapter 2 for more explanation.)

2. You are familiar enough with this language that you can:

  i. define a list (or other collection type) that will play a critical role in fulfilling the goal of your program.

   ‣ for this key list, you can:

    – explain the data stored in the list

    – identify where in the code the list is being used

  ii. define a procedure that plays an important role in accomplishing the purpose of your program.

   ‣ for this key procedure, you can:

    – be sure it has at least one parameter

    – define the data type of the input(s) to the procedure

    – define the data type of the output(s) from the procedure

    – explain why sequence (order) matters in the procedure

Test Tip *Besides lists, other examples of collection types include: arrays, databases, hash tables, dictionaries, and sets.*

- – explain why selection (conditional statement(s) such as if, else-if, else) matters in the procedure

- – explain why iteration (loops such as for, while) matters in the procedure

- – explain how you tested the procedure to be sure it worked for at least two different code segments

- – explain how you designed the procedure to have one or more parameters that have an effect on the functionality of the program

3. You have an idea for your task. (See Chapter 3.)

4. You have started your journal. (See Chapter 3.)

 II. **UNDERSTAND HOW YOUR PROGRAM SUPPORTS YOUR CREATE PERFORMANCE TASK**

A. The planning and work that you do to create your final program is part of each question that you will answer for your Create Performance Task.

B. To get full credit, your Create Performance Task submission needs to show that you completed all of the following:

1. You did what you planned to do. This means one of the following:

   i. You solved the problem you set out to solve.

   ii. You created something that is entertaining for people to use.

iii. You created a program that will help someone to better understand something.

2. You used approaches to design that have led to your creation of:

   i.   a key list that manages complexity.

   ii. a key procedure, with parameters, that you have tested.

C. Keep in mind that your Create Performance Task write-up is connected to the program in the following ways:

   1. In Prompt 1, you hand in a PDF of all of your program code as well as any citations.

   2. In Prompt 2, you submit a video that demonstrates the running of your program. This video will be the introduction to your first written response prompt. The video should show the purpose and function of your program as well as the input to and output from the program.

   3. In Prompt 3a, parts i-iii, you will write about the purpose, functionality, and the input to and output from the program in your video.

   4. In Prompt 3b, parts i-v, you will write about the key list for your program. You will share two code segments.

      i.   In **i**, the code segment will show how data was stored in the list.

      ii. In **ii**, the code segment will show the data in the same list being used to fulfill the program's purpose.

      iii. In **iii**, you will identify the name of the list.

      iv. In **iv**, you will describe what the data in the list does for your program.

      v.   In **v**, you will explain how the key list manages a complexity by writing about why the list is necessary for your code to function or how the program would be different if the list was not there.

5. In Prompt 3c, parts i–iv, you will focus on the key procedure you wrote for the program. You will share two segments.

    i. In **i**, the code segment will show an important and strong procedure you created.

    ii. In **ii**, the code segment will show where your procedure is being called in the program.

    iii. In **iii**, you will describe what the procedure does and how it contributes to the functionality of the program.

    iv. In **iv**, you will write about how the procedure works with enough detail that someone reading your description could recreate the procedure.

6. In Prompt 3d, parts i–iii, you will explain how you tested the key procedure from Prompt 3c. When you write your responses to Prompt 3d, you will be referring to the code you shared in Prompt 3c.

    i. In **i**, you will explain two different calls to the procedure with two different arguments to the procedure. Each call must cause the procedure to execute a different code segment.

    ii. In **ii**, you will write about the condition being tested by each of these calls to the procedure.

    iii. In **iii**, you will identify the result of each call to the procedure.

Test Tip

Notice how the Software Development Cycle is showing up in these prompts: idea, design, implement, test.

D. Keep the following in mind: As you work through this task, remember that your program is the centerpiece of your Create Performance Task and that it is important that you have a plan in place to manage your time.

III. MANAGING YOUR TIME

A. Once you know a language and have a design plan, the most challenging part of the Create Performance Task is managing your time. This section assumes you:

1. know a programming language.

2. have an idea and a design.

3. are ready to devote time to writing your program.

B. Implementing a program requires flexibility. Changes are common. However, if you decide to change a key idea for your program or a major piece of your design, you may need more time than is shown here.

Hour	Goals	Managing Common Issues	Additional Information that Should Be in Your Journal*
1	You have an idea and a design plan. The idea will require a list (or other collection type) and a procedure that will have at least one parameter. You have started your plan and you know enough programming that you are ready to start coding.	Issue 1: You are having trouble seeing where the list will be useful. – To solve this, look for items that will come in groups for your idea. What are the collections of things that your program will need? – If you cannot find a collection in your current idea, you will need a new idea and a new design for this task. It is good you caught this now!	What is the purpose of your program? What are the major challenges to your design and how will you fix this? If you are working with someone else, how will you manage this? What will your key list be called and what will it do for your program? What is a likely procedure? What parameter will it take? What will it do? How is this procedure going to help you fulfill the purpose of your program?

(continued)

* See the end of Chapter 3 to review what needs to be included in your journal entries.

Hour	Goals	Managing Common Issues	Additional Information that Should Be in Your Journal*
		Issue 2: You cannot see where a procedure with a parameter will be useful. – To solve this, look at the problem(s) your code is trying to solve. Look for repeated behaviors or an action that will have different outcomes, based on inputs. – It is possible that the procedure will become more clear as you code. However, keep this requirement in the back of your mind. – If you are nearing the end of your program design and you still do not have a procedure with a parameter, you may need to add more features to your program to justify adding a parameter.	

Hour	Goals	Managing Common Issues	Additional Information that Should Be in Your Journal*
2	You complete your initial coding structure. Methods or procedures might be missing their bodies, but they are being called where they should be. The order makes sense and aligns with your design. (Note: this is one of several ideas for how to begin.)	Issue: You are not sure where to begin. – To solve this, try to step away from the code and focus on your design. – Remember, your list should be present. – Focus on writing one method or debugging one thing.	What will your key list be called and what will it do for your program? What procedure is emerging as a possible key procedure? What parameter will it take? What will it do? How is this procedure going to help you fulfill the purpose of your program?
3	If you have not already done so, name and create your key list.	Issue: You are not sure how the list will be created for your code. Maybe you are deciding between a user inputting it or if it will come from a data file. – To solve this, create a list that mimics the way it will eventually exist in your code. Then use this to test your code until you have time to build code that generates a list, if needed. (Note: The list might be a static set of values that is not changing and that is fine, too.)	What is your key list being called? What type of data is stored in this list? Why is this list necessary or helpful in your program? If it was not there, what would be the impact on your program?

(continued)

Hour	Goals	Managing Common Issues	Additional Information that Should Be in Your Journal*
4–5	Write and test the key procedure that will be your focus in Prompts 3c and 3d of the written response. Name your procedure something that is meaningful in your program. The name should be related to what the procedure is doing in your program. Be sure it is complex enough. It should: – be called in your program to do something vital – have at least one parameter that affects how the procedure works – include sequence, selection, and iteration – be created by you or another student collaboratively	Issue: You find a bug in the procedure through testing. – To solve this, use debugging tools you learned with your programming language. – Every 3–4 lines of code, you should test to be sure it is working the way you intended.	How does this procedure connect to the purpose and function of your program? What parameter will it take? What will it do? How is this procedure going to help you fulfill the purpose of your program? What is this procedure called? What other procedures do you need to write? How did you test that this procedure works? What two (or more) inputs did you try? What happened in the code to prove that the procedure executed a different part of the code when each input was used?

Hour	Goals	Managing Common Issues	Additional Information that Should Be in Your Journal*
5–6	Write the other procedures. Test your code frequently. Note that writing these procedures may happen at the same time that you are writing your key procedure.	Issue: You have written several lines of code and waited to test. Now you cannot tell where the issue came from in your code. – To solve this, comment out code you created in order until you have only 3–4 lines of code to test. Then test and fix 3–4 lines at a time.	By the end of Hour 6, you should be done with coding and you should be ready to work on the final submission for your Create Task. If not, your Journal Entry should be focused on this. Here are some ideas for prompts: What do you still need to accomplish? How long will this take? How will you find the time to do this?

IV. FINDING IMAGES FOR YOUR PROGRAM

A. Your program does not have to involve images, but if it does, you should be careful with how you are using internet search results to find images.

B. Not all images found should be used in your application. Whenever possible, you should use Creative Commons sources for images.

Test Tip

Creative Commons images are preferred to images found through unfiltered search results because the creator has given permission and details for how to use their images.

C. You will need to create a citation for any image that you used in the program that you did not create yourself.

1. If the image came from a Creative Commons Source such as Wikimedia Commons, most images have an explanation for how they should be cited. You should use the approach specified by the author.

2. If you need to create a citation, you will need the following: a description of the image, the image link, the date you retrieved the image, and the title of the webpage where you found the image. If known, the name of the person who created the image and the image title would be ideal.

3. You can use a tool like NoodleTools.com to create citations or you can type them manually.

4. The citation will likely look something like this:

    i. Last name, First name (of person who created image). "Title of image." Website Title. Website Publisher. Website URL. Date you retrieved image.

    ii. To the left of "Last name," you should label the citation with a description of the image (something like, "image in top right corner" or some other type of brief description so your reader can tell which citation goes with which image).

When you find an image you know you will be using, save time and create the citation right then and there. Put these citations in a document for safe-keeping. You will need them in Chapter 5.

V. SELF-ASSESSMENT

A. You will know you are ready to begin working on submitting your program code, video, and written response when you can respond "yes" to each of the following questions. These are the questions that graders will ask themselves when they view your program code, watch your video, and read your response to decide if you should earn full credit.

Question	Yes	No
1. Does your program fulfill a purpose?		
2. Think of the key list you focused on in your program. Then answer these questions about that list: ▸ Does the list represent a collection of data in your program? ▸ Is this list necessary for your code to work? If not, would your program be written differently without this list? ▸ Does the list help to fulfill the purpose of the program?		
3. Think of the key procedure that you wrote and plan to highlight. ▸ Does the procedure have one or more parameters (inputs)? ▸ Can you explain why sequencing, selection, and iteration are used in this procedure? ▸ Do you call the procedure? ▸ Do the behaviors of this procedure depend on the input? (Do different segments of code run when the input changes?) ▸ Can you explain how this procedure fulfills the purpose of the program? ▸ Did you write this procedure yourself or collaboratively with another person?		

Program Code: Submission Requirement 1

I. OVERVIEW

A. At this point you should have completed the following actions in your Create Performance Task:

1. You have decided on a programming language. (See Chapter 2 for more explanation.)

2. You created a design based on a programming idea. (See Chapter 3.)

3. You used your programming knowledge to translate your idea into a program. (See Chapter 4.)

Test Tip

If you have not already done so, you should view the Create Performance Task Requirements in Appendix A and the Create Performance Task Checklist in Appendix B. Submitting your code is one of several steps required to submit a successful task. Reviewing the task will help you to understand how this step fits into the whole task.

B. You are now ready to work on the items you will be handing in to the College Board to complete your Create Performance Task.

1. The first item you need to create is a PDF of your Program Code. That is the focus for this chapter.

2. The second item you will need is a video of your program running. Details for this item are provided in Chapter 6.

3. The third item is your written response to Prompts 3a-3d. This is the focus of Chapters 7–10.

Test Tip

You do not have to complete the items above in the order they're listed. By first considering how you want to respond to the prompts, you may find that you are able to devise a better idea for the program you need to design and create to satisfy the requirements of the task.

II. **TIPS FOR HOW TO ORGANIZE AND CREATE YOUR PROGRAM CODE PDF**

A. There is no word count or page limit for your program code. Use this to your advantage to hand in an organized final product. Steps 1–9 below will walk you through exactly how to do this.

1. Create a document. Open up any document editor. You can use Google Docs, Microsoft Word, Pages, or any equivalent.

2. Put the following Title on the top of page 1: "Program Code."

3. If your programming environment allows you to include comments, use this to credit another author.

   i. If you found code on the internet that you added to for this project, include the name of the author, title of source code (if available), website title, web address or publisher (if you used a book), and end with the date you retrieved your code.

   ii. The citation will look something like this: Last name, First name (of person who created code). "Title of source code." Website Title. Website Publisher. Website URL. Date you retrieved code.

 iii. If the person you are citing is your coding partner, write, "My partner completed this code" in the comments.

  ▸ The person reading your code will know that this means that you did not complete this code.

  ▸ You should not put your partner's name in the code, nor should you ever write your name in the code.

  ▸ If you and your partner collaborated to create your code, then you do not need to cite it.

Test Tip

 You can use code developed cooperatively in the written response. However, you and your partner would each be creating your own video and writing your own written response.

4. Take screenshots of your code.

 i. Most computers come with at least one tool to help you take pictures of your screen.

  ▸ For PC users, there is a "Snipping Tool." Press the windows icon in the bottom left corner of your screen and type, "snip".

  ▸ For Mac users, press Shift, Command, and 4 together.

  ▸ Lightshot is a popular tool you can download to most operating systems.

 ii. Drag the rectangle around the area you want to capture. This will create an image you can copy and paste into this document.

 iii. Put all of your code here using as many pages as needed.

 iv. Be sure to keep the code you created yourself separate from the code someone else created.

 v. Be sure your code is readable. Code font size should be at least 10 point and images should be clear enough to read easily.

5. Create code citations (only needed if you could not use comments to cite your code).

    i.   If you could not use comments to cite your code in your development environment, put numbers on or near the code you did not complete yourself. These numbers will be used to create your citations.

    ii. Hit "Enter" a few times after the last section of code. Type: "Code Citations".

    iii. List your citations. Put a number to the left of the citation to indicate the code being cited.

6. Create your image citations.

    i.   Hit "Enter" a few times after the coding section to start creating your image citations.

    ii. Title this part of the document, "Image Citations."

    iii. You will need to create a citation for any image that you used in the program that you did not create yourself.

       ▸ If the image came from a Creative Commons source such as Wikimedia Commons, it will most likely come with an explanation for how it should be cited. You should use the approach specified by the author.

       ▸ If you need to create a citation, be sure to include a description of the image, the image link, the date you retrieved the image, and the title of the webpage where you found the image. If known, the name of the person who created the image and the image title would be ideal.

          – The citation will likely look something like this:

             a. Last name, First name (of person who created image). "Title of image." Website Title. Website Publisher. Website URL. Date you retrieved image.

       b. To the left of "Last name," label the citation with a description of the image (something like, "image in top right corner" or some other type of brief description so your reader can tell which citation goes with which image).

7. Change your program code document to a PDF.

    i. From your document editor, choose File, then Print.

    ii. There should be a print option that includes a PDF printer. Choose that. In Google Docs, you can choose File, then Download, then Download as a PDF. There is also a Google Chrome Extension you can use on Chromebooks to create PDFs.

8. Find your PDF file.

    i. The PDF file will be stored on your computer or on the internet.

    ii. Follow directions provided by the software you used to create the PDF to retrieve this file.

    iii. This file is what you will need to hand in for the first part of your Create Task.

III. SELF-ASSESSMENT

A. You will know you are ready to begin working on your video and written response when you can respond "yes" to each of the following questions.

Question	Yes	No
1. Does your program code appear organized?		
2. Is all of your program code included in this final product?		
3. Did you cite any code you did not create yourself or help to create?		

(continued)

Question	Yes	No
4. Did you cite any images you did not create yourself?		
5. Did you convert this document to a PDF?		

Congratulations! This Program Code PDF is the first of three items you will need to submit to the Digital Portfolio to complete your Create Performance Task. Save the document and the PDF some place safe and move on to Chapter 6 to create your video.

Video: Submission Requirement 2

I. OVERVIEW

A. When you submit the Create Performance Task to the College Board via the Digital Portfolio, upload the following three items:

1. A PDF of your entire Program Code, including any image or code citations.

2. A video of your program showing the purpose, behavior, input to, and output from the program.

3. Your responses to Prompts 3a–3d.

B. This chapter focuses on the creation of your video to showcase that your program takes input, does something related to its purpose, and produces output.

II. PLANNING TO RECORD THE VIDEO

A. Your video needs to show all of the following in less than one minute:

1. the input to the program

2. that your program is doing something related to its purpose

3. the output produced by the program

B. Using Your Video to Show Your Program's Input

1. The input to the program should come from one of the following:

   i.   a user (including actions that cause events to occur in the program, like pressing a button)

   ii. a device

   iii. an online data stream

   iv. a file

2. Plan to start your video recording before this input happens in the program to be sure it is captured.

C. Using Your Video to Show Your Program's Behavior

1. Think about the purpose of your program.

2. Your video should show that, as a result of the input, your program is doing something connected to the program's purpose.

3. If you have time, consider changing the inputs to show that the program does something different depending on the input.

D. Using Your Video to Show Your Program's Output

1. The output could be sent to any of the following:

   i.   the user (via the main screen of the program or a separate window)

   ii. a device

   iii. an online data stream

   iv. a file

2. The output is the resulting behavior of the program.

3. Plan to end your video recording after at least one output is shown.

Having a plan before you record will save you time during the actual recording process and it will make it more likely that your video will show what it needs to show to earn credit.

III. RECORDING THE VIDEO

A. Keep these guidelines in mind when you are ready to record your video:

1. This video is what graders will view to see what your Create Performance Task looks like in action.

   i. Make it professional.

      ▸ Use screen-capture software such as Screencast-O-Matic or equivalent to record your program running on a typical computer.

      ▸ If your program is running on a smartphone, use screen-capture software that is on your phone or can be found as a free download.

      ▸ If you must record your program on your phone (if your program is used to make a robot move, for example), use a stabilizer to prevent the image from shaking and record in landscape mode.

   ii. Use images that are school appropriate. Avoid violence, etc.

   iii. The video must be unbroken.

      ▸ It can be edited for size.

      ▸ The beginning and/or end of the video can be removed if needed.

2. Your video must be recorded using .mp4, .wmv, .avi, or .mov format. The video cannot exceed 1 minute in length or 30 MB in size. The following tools and tips may be helpful:

i. Control the resolution of the video before you record. By default, recorders may use a resolution that is higher than you need.

ii. Use video-editing software such as WeVideo (*WeVideo. com*) to shorten the video or save it using a smaller format.

iii. Use video compression software such as Clipchamp (*ClipChamp.com*) to decrease the resolution of the video after it has been recorded.

iv. If your program does not run in a visual way (for example, your program causes music to play), use another tool to make the video more effective. Examples of helpful tools in this case are:

  ‣ Animoto (*animoto.com*), which turns still images into a video. You can also add text. You could add this music as audio to this video.

  ‣ You could create a presentation using the software Prezi (*prezi.com*) to run automatically at the same time as the sound.

v. If you need to edit sound files, *Audacity (audacityteam. org)* or any other sound editor will help you to modify the sound.

B. Here are some things to avoid when recording your video:

1. Do not show your code unless it is necessary in the development environment you are using.

   i. You already showed all of your code in the Program Code PDF for the task.

   ii. You will show key pieces of your code in the Written Response section of the task.

2. Do not narrate your video.

   i. You will explain choices you made for the video in the Written Response section of the task.

    ii.   Graders will not award points for anything you say or any text you add to your video.

  3. Do not put your name or any self-identifying information in the video.

III. SELF-ASSESSMENT

A. Now, take the time to show this video to someone else. After they have viewed it, ask yourself the questions listed below. If you do not answer "yes" to any of the questions here, take the time to remake your video.

Question	Yes	No
1. Did they see the program receive input from a user, device, online data stream, or file?		
2. Did the video show the program doing something connected to its purpose after receiving the input?		
3. Did the video show the program producing an output?		
4. Was the video less than 1 minute in length?		
5. Is the video smaller than 30 MB in size?		

Congratulations! This video is the second of three items you will need to submit to the Digital Portfolio to complete your Create Performance Task. Save this video file in a safe place and move on to Chapter 7 to begin the Written Responses.

Written Response to Prompt 3a: Introducing Your Program

I. OVERVIEW

A. When you submit your Create Performance Task to the College Board via the Digital Portfolio, you will upload the following three items:

1. a PDF of your program code, including any citations

2. a video of your program showing the purpose, behavior, input to, and output from the program

3. your responses to Prompts 3a–3d

B. This chapter will focus on your written response to Prompt 3a in which you describe the key aspects of the program that you captured in your video. You will find discussions of the remaining Prompts 3b, 3c, and 3d in Chapters 8, 9, and 10.

II. TIPS FOR WRITING RESPONSES TO PROMPTS 3a–3d

A. Here are some tips that will save you time when writing your responses to any of the prompts in the Create Performance Task:

1. Keep your program as the focus for all prompts.

2. Create a folder to hold your responses.

    i. You will copy and paste all of your responses into the Digital Portfolio when you are ready to submit.

     ii. Name your folders and files carefully. Some responses have many parts, so how you name your files and folders will make a big difference in your ability to find what you need to find to complete this task.

3. Setting up your file structure:

     i. If you have not already done so, create a folder on your computer, on your school's network, or in an online storage environment like Dropbox or Google Drive. Call the main folder: "Create PT"

     ii. Double-click to go into your new "Create PT" folder and add the following six items to that folder:

- ▶ The Program Code PDF you created (See Chapter 5.)
- ▶ The Video File you recorded (See Chapter 6.)
- ▶ A folder called "Prompt 3a"
- ▶ A folder called "Prompt 3b"
- ▶ A folder called "Prompt 3c"
- ▶ A folder called "Prompt 3d"

Test Tip

When creating a response in the Digital Portfolio's online form, you should not directly type your responses there. Make a separate folder with these responses in case something goes wrong during the online submission.

B. Watch the word-count limit for each prompt.

C. Refer to the following often as you write:

1. The writing prompts for the Create Performance Task in Appendix C.

2. The Scoring Guidelines for the Create Performance Task in Appendix D. You can find the full guidelines on AP® Central here: *apcentral.collegeboard.org*

3. Your journal notes.

III. **PROMPT 3a (INTRODUCING YOUR PROGRAM)**

A. Both the video and your response to Prompt 3a are required to earn credit for this prompt.

1. Your video needs to show all of the following:

   i. input to your program—what starts the program

   ii. program functionality—what the program does with that input

   iii. output from your program

2. Your written response needs to include a description of all of the following:

   i. the purpose of the program

   ii. the functionality that was shown in the video

   iii. the input and output of the program demonstrated in the video

B. Remember, this is the prompt that connects your video to the written responses.

Remember that you can only use code you completed or helped to complete to answer the prompts in the written response. Cited code that you did not help to create may not be used in the written response.

IV. **SETTING UP FOR PROMPT 3a**

A. Here is what the prompt will look like in the online template. The large rectangular boxes are here to show you where, in the online form, you will need to paste your responses.

3a. Provide a written response that does all three of the following:

Approximately 150 words (for all subparts of 3a combined)

i. Describes the overall purpose of the program

ii. Describes what functionality of the program is demonstrated in the video

iii. Describes the input and output of the program demonstrated in the video

B. Use your favorite word-processing software to create a document that has space for all three responses. Then put that document inside the "Prompt 3a" folder.

V. KEY ASPECTS OF PROMPT 3a

A. In Prompt 3a, you have 150 words (or less) to:

1. describe the overall purpose of the program.

2. describe the functionality of the program that is demonstrated in the video.

3. describe the input and output of the program demonstrated in the video.

Test Tip

The video, combined with prompt 3a, is worth 1 point out of 6 possible points for the Create Performance Task.

B. To maximize your credit for Prompt 3a, do the following:

1. Refer to your journal and watch your video again.

2. Start writing by answering Prompt i as briefly and clearly as you can.

    i. Use 1 sentence to explain why you created your program.

    ii. Your response should answer the following question: Why did you create your program?

3. After you have responded to Prompt i, move on to Prompt ii.

    i. Use 1–2 sentences to describe the functionality of the program being demonstrated in the video.

    ii. Your response should answer the following question: What is your program doing in the video?

4. Part iii is the third and final prompt you need to write for Prompt 3a.

    i. Use 1 sentence to describe the inputs to your program.

    ii. Use 1 sentence to describe the outputs produced by the program.

    iii. Your response should answer the following questions: What starts the program? What does the program produce that a user can see?

Test Tip

In each of your written responses 3a–3d, include the language from the Create Performance Task Prompt to help your reader find your response and understand your intent. For Part i of Prompt 3a, for example, begin the answer to this prompt with: "The purpose of my program is to. . . ." Then state specifically what problem you solved, what you were studying, or what you were trying to create.

C. Remember to save your responses in the "Prompt 3a" folder so you will have it when you are finished with answering all of the prompts.

VI. SELF-ASSESSMENT

A. When you view your video and read your final written response to Prompt 3a, be sure you are able to answer "yes" to each of the following questions. If not, revise your response to maximize your score. These are the questions that graders will ask themselves when they read your response to decide whether you should earn full credit for your response.

Question	Yes	No
Look at your video. Then answer these questions about your video: ▸ Does your video show your program running? ▸ In the video, can you see the program's input? This could be any of the following: user's actions, another device, data stream or data file. ▸ In the video, can you see the program's functionality? ▸ In the video, can you see the program's output?		
Look at your written response to prompt 3a. Then answer your questions about your response: ▸ In part i, do you describe the overall purpose of the program? ▸ In part ii, do you describe the functionality of the program demonstrated in the video? ▸ In part iii, do you describe the input and output of the program shown in the video?		

Congratulations! Prompt 3a is the start of your written responses to the Create Task. Save the document you created to hold your responses someplace safe and move on to Chapter 8 to work on Prompt 3b.

Written Response to Prompt 3b: Key List in Your Program

OVERVIEW

A. Prompt 3b asks you to share two code segments and write three written responses about the key list (or any other collection type) that you used in your program.

B. To get full credit for this prompt, you need to do all of the following:

1. Share two different code segments.

    i. The first segment needs to show how data is stored in the list.

    ii. The second segment needs to show the data being used in a meaningful way to fulfill the program's purpose.

2. Write three different responses to answer the following prompts in 200 words or less:

    i. The first prompt asks you to identify the name of the list.

    ii. The second prompt asks you to describe the data stored in the list.

    iii. The third prompt asks you to explain how the list manages complexity.

II. **SETTING UP FOR PROMPT 3B**

A. Here is what the prompt will look like in the online template. The large rectangular boxes show you where you will paste your responses in the online form.

3b. Capture and paste two program code segments you developed during the administration of this task that contain a list (or other collection type) being used to manage complexity in your program.

    i.   The first program code segment must show how data have been stored in the list.

_____

    ii. The second program code segment must show the data in the same list being used, such as creating new data from the existing data or accessing multiple elements in the list, as part of fulfilling the program's purpose.

_____

Then, provide a written response that does all three of the following:

    iii. Identifies the name of the list being used in this response

_____

    iv. Describes what the data contained in the list represent in your program

_____

    v.   Explains how the selected list manages complexity in your program code by explaining why your program code could not be written, or how it would be written differently, if you did not use the list

_____

B. Use your favorite word-processing software and create a document that has space for parts iii, iv, and v. Then put that document inside the "Prompt 3b" folder.

III. HOW TO MAXIMIZE YOUR SCORE WHILE WRITING ABOUT YOUR KEY LIST

A. Stay under the word count. You have 200 words to write parts iii, iv, and v.

B. Refer to your journal. This is your chance to highlight the key list you planned to use in your program.

C. Remember that the list can be any collection type.

1. A collection type is any data type that collects elements into a single structure.

2. Examples include: lists, arrays, arraylists, databases, hash tables, dictionaries, and sets.

Code font size should be 10 point or larger. You want your readers to be able to read your code easily!

D. To complete part i, you will upload an image of your code that shows data being stored in the key list.

1. At the end of the code segment you share in part i, your list needs to have data stored in it.

2. For now, use a snipping tool to save that code as an image called "part i." Put this image in the "Prompt 3b" folder.

E. To complete part ii, you will upload an image of your code that shows data stored in the key list being used in some significant way to fulfill your program's purpose.

1. Some examples of significant ways to use a list are:

i. The list is used to create new data from the existing data in the program.

ii. Multiple elements from the list are being accessed in the program.

2. The code you share in part ii should show the list being used so that you are showing that the list is necessary for the program to work or it is making something easier in your program.

3. For now, use a snipping tool to save that code as an image called "part ii." Put this image in the "Prompt 3b" folder.

Remember to open the document you created in the "Prompt 3b" folder to create your responses to parts iii, iv, and v.

F. To complete part iii, you will write 1 sentence to identify the name of the list being used in this response.

G. To complete part iv, write 1–2 sentences to describe what the data stored in the list represent in the program.

1. The name you chose for the list should align with the meaning of the list in your program.

2. Suppose, for example, you created a series of card objects to represent a deck of cards and you stored those cards in some sort of data collection. Then the collection should be called "deck" or "cards."

Through the name you chose for the list, you should have made the connection between parts iii and iv easier to explain. In part iii you state the name. Part iv justifies (explains) the name in the context of the whole program.

H. To complete part v, you need to write about how the list manages complexity in your program code. To get full credit for this response you need to do *one* of the following:

  1. Explain why the program code could not be written if you did not use the list.

  2. Explain how the program code would be written differently if you did not use the list.

Prompt 3b is worth 2 points out of 6 possible points for the Create Performance Task. The first of these points comes from the written responses in iii and iv. The second of these points comes from part v. All written responses in iii, iv, and v refer to the key list code segments shared in parts i and ii.

IV. SELF-ASSESSMENT

A. When you view your code segments and read your final written responses to Prompt 3b, be sure you are able to answer "yes" to each of the following questions. If not, revise your response to maximize your score. These are the questions that graders will ask themselves when they read your response to decide whether you should earn full credit for your response.

Question	Yes	No
1. Are all of your responses to prompt 3b about the list or other collection type shown in parts i and ii?		

2. Look at your code segments in parts i and ii. Then answer the following questions about the code segments:
  ▸ Did you develop or help to develop both code segments?
  ▸ Does the segment you used for part i show how data has been stored in the list?		

(continued)

Question	Yes	No
▸ Does the segment you used for part ii show how the data is being used in your program as part of fulfilling the program's purpose? ▸ Can you tell that the list is either (1) necessary for your code to work or (2) is helping your code to work more efficiently?		
3. Look at your written response in parts iii and iv. Then answer the following questions about these two parts of your written response. ▸ In part iii, do you identify the name of the variable representing the list being used in the response? ▸ In part iv, do you describe what the data in this list is representing in the program?		
4. Look at your written response in part v. Then answer the following questions about this part of your written response. ▸ Can you see how the list is managing complexity in the code segments shown in parts i and ii? ▸ In part v, do you describe how the named, selected list manages complexity by explaining why the program code could not be written, or how it would be written differently, without using this list?		

Congratulations! Prompt 3b is the second prompt of your written responses to the Create Task. Save the images for parts i and ii and the document you created to hold your responses to parts iii–iv someplace safe and move on to Chapter 9 to work on Prompt 3c.

Written Response to Prompt 3c: Key Procedure in Your Program

OVERVIEW

A. Prompt 3c asks you to share two code segments and write two written responses about the key procedure that you used in your program.

B. To get full credit for this prompt, you need to do all of the following:

1. Share two different code segments.

   i. The first segment needs to show a procedure that you developed independently or collaboratively.

   ii. The second segment needs to show where the procedure is being called.

2. Write two different responses to answer the following prompts in 200 words or less.

   i. The first prompt asks you to describe (generally) what the program does and how it contributes to the program.

   ii. The second prompt asks you to explain in detailed steps how the algorithm works.

II. SETTING UP FOR PROMPT 3C

A. Here is what the prompt will look like in the online template. The large rectangular boxes show where you will paste your responses in the online form.

3c. Capture and paste two program code segments you developed during the administration of this task that contain a student-developed procedure that implements an algorithm used in your program and a call to that procedure.

Approx. 200 words (for all subparts of 3c combined, exclusive of program code)

   i. The first program code segment must be a student-developed procedure that:

- Defines the procedure's name and return type (if necessary).

- Contains and uses one or more parameters that have an effect on the functionality of the procedure.

- Implements an algorithm that includes sequencing, selection, and iteration.

        [ ]

   ii. The second program code segment must show where your student-developed procedure is being called in your program.

        [ ]

Then, provide a written response that does both of the following:

   iii. Describes in general what the identified procedure does and how it contributes to the overall functionality of the program.

        [ ]

   iv. Explains in detailed steps how the algorithm implemented in the identified procedure works. Your explanation must be detailed enough for someone else to recreate it.

        [ ]

B. Use your favorite word-processing software and create a document that has space for parts iii, iv, and v. Then put that document inside the "Prompt 3c" folder.

Remember that even if you collaborated to create your code with a coding partner, you must each create your own images and write your own written responses to all writing prompts.

III. HOW TO MAXIMIZE YOUR SCORE WHILE WRITING ABOUT YOUR KEY PROCEDURE

A. Stay under the word count. You have 200 words to write parts iii and iv.

B. Refer to your journal. This is your chance to highlight the key procedure you planned to use in your program.

C. Remember that the following things must be true about the procedure shared in part i:

1. The procedure must be student developed.

2. The entire procedure should be shown, including the name and return type (if that is needed for the language you are using).

3. The procedure should contain and use one or more parameters.

4. These parameters should impact how the procedure behaves.

5. The procedure should show all of the following:

   i.   sequencing—order should matter in some part of the code

   ii. selection—conditional statements such as an if statement need to be present and used

      iii. iteration—looping should be required to accomplish something in this procedure

  6. You need to be able to explain this procedure using detailed steps so someone viewing your explanation could recreate the procedure.

D. To complete part i, you will upload an image of your code that shows your key procedure.

  1. This code needs to be developed by you or collaboratively with your partner.

  2. You should include your entire procedure.

  3. Code font size should be 10 point or larger.

  4. For now, use a snipping tool to save that code as an image called "part i." Put this image in the "Prompt 3c" folder.

E. To complete part ii, you will upload an image of your code showing where you are calling the procedure in part i.

  1. The code you share in part ii should show the procedure being called to do something significant for your program.

  2. For now, use a snipping tool to save that code as an image called "part ii." Put this image in the "Prompt 3c" folder.

F. To complete part iii, you will write 1 sentence to describe generally what the procedure is doing for your program.

  1. You need not get into the details of how the procedure works. Instead, describe what the procedure does as if you are talking to someone who does not know much about programming.

  2. Connect to the purpose and overall function of your program.

G. To complete part iv, write 4–5 sentences about how the program works.

    1. You should get into the details here. You can assume your reader knows how to program.

    2. In fact, steps should be detailed enough that someone reading your explanation should be able to recreate the procedure you created.

> *Prompt 3c is worth 2 points out of 6 possible points for the Create Performance Task. The first of these points comes from the written responses in iii. The second of these points comes from part iv. All written responses in iii and iv refer to the key procedure code segments shared in parts i and ii.*

IV. SELF-ASSESSMENT

A. When you view your code segments and read your final written responses to Prompt 3c, be sure you are able to answer "yes" to each of the following questions. If not, revise your response to maximize your score. These are the questions that graders will ask themselves when they read your response to decide whether you should earn full credit for your response.

Question	Yes	No
1. Are all of your responses to prompt 3c about the key procedure shown in parts i and ii?		

2. Look at your code segments in parts i and ii. Then answer the following questions about the code segments:
 	
  ▸ Did you develop or help to develop both code segments?
 	
  ▸ Does the segment you used for part i show at least one parameter that has an effect on how the procedure works?		

(continued)

Question	Yes	No
▸ Does the segment you used for part ii show where the procedure is being called? ▸ Can you see that order (sequencing) matters in the procedure shown? ▸ Can you see where conditional statements (selection) is used in the key procedure? ▸ Can you see that looping (iteration) is necessary in this key procedure?		
3. Look at your written response in part iii. Then answer the following questions about this part of your written response. ▸ Do you describe generally what the procedure does? ▸ Do you explain how the procedure helps to make the whole program work?		
4. Look at your written response in part iv. Then answer the following questions about this part of your written response. ▸ Can you see sequencing, selection, and iteration in the code segment shown in part i? ▸ Do you explain, using detailed steps, how the procedure works using enough detail that someone else could recreate it?		

Congratulations on completing Prompt 3c! Prompt 3c is the third prompt of your written responses to the Create Task. Save the images for parts i and ii and the document you created to hold your responses to parts iii-iv someplace safe and move on to Chapter 10 to work on Prompt 3d.

Written Response to Prompt 3d: Testing Your Key Procedure

10

I. OVERVIEW

A. Prompt 3d asks you to write six written responses about how you tested the key procedure that you used in your program.

B. Your responses to Prompt 3d will refer back to the code segments you shared in Prompt 3c.

C. To get full credit for this prompt, you need to do all of the following:

1. Use 200 words or less to handle all six responses.

2. Explain two distinct calls to the procedure, each using different arguments.

3. Describe the condition(s) tested by each of these calls to the procedure.

4. Identify the result of each of these calls to the procedure.

II. SETTING UP FOR PROMPT 3D

A. Here is what the prompt will look like in the online template. The large rectangular boxes show you where you will paste your responses in the online form.

3d. Provide a written response that does all three of the following:

Approx. 200 words (for all subparts of 3d combined)

1. Describes two calls to the procedure identified in written response 3c. Each call must pass a different argument(s) that causes a different segment of code in the algorithm to execute.

   First call:

   Second call:

2. Describes what condition(s) is being tested by each call to the procedure.

   Condition(s) tested by the first call:

   Condition(s) tested by the second call:

3. Identifies the result of each call.

   Result of the first call:

   Result of the second call:

B. Use your favorite word-processing software and create a document that has space for parts iii, iv, and v. Then put that document inside the "Prompt 3d" folder.

III. HOW TO MAXIMIZE YOUR SCORE WHILE WRITING ABOUT TESTING YOUR KEY PROCEDURE

A. Stay under the word count. You have 200 words to write parts i–iii.

B. Refer to your journal. This is your chance to show why you know your key procedure works.

C. Remember that the following things must be true about your response to Prompt 3d:

1. You are writing about the key procedure you identified and described in parts i and ii in Prompt 3c.

2. Do not over explain. You should be able to answer the six different parts by writing no more than 1–2 sentences for each.

3. When you describe the two calls, choose those calls carefully. Be sure that each call passes a different argument that causes a different part of the code to execute.

An argument is an actual value being used to replace a parameter in a procedure call. For example, if you wrote a procedure called doSomething(x), *x is a parameter. If you call that procedure, the call may look like this:* doSomething(5). *For that call, 5 is the argument.*

D. To complete part i, you will explain two different calls to your key procedure.

1. Each call must satisfy *both* of the following requirements:

   i. Each call must use a different argument.

   ii. Each call must cause a different segment of code in the algorithm to execute.

2. You are not sharing you code here. Instead you are *explaining* the calls in words.

3. For each rectangle in part i, do the following:

   i. Share what the procedure call looks like. (Name the procedure and the argument.)

   ii. Explain what the code does broadly, as if you are writing this for someone who does not know how to program.

E. To complete part ii, you will explain the conditions being tested by each call to the procedure.

1. In the first rectangle, you will explain the condition(s) being tested by the first call you provided in part i.

2. In the second rectangle, you will explain the condition(s) being tested by the second call provided in part i.

Test Tip

> *A condition is something that has a Boolean result, so it is true or false. Examples of statements using a condition are: if, else if, or else statements. Loops (while, for, etc.) also have conditions that are evaluated (as true or false) in each iteration of the loop. Both types of conditions would work for part ii.*

3. For each rectangle in part ii, do the following:

   i.   Share what the procedure call looked like by naming the procedure and the argument.

   ii. Explain what part of the code this argument will reach because, for this argument, the condition is true.

   iii. Explain what part of the code this argument will reach that the other argument will not reach. Do not mention the other argument, but explain why the condition is true for this argument.

Remember that Prompt 3d is about testing your key procedure. It is important that you explain the parts of the algorithm that each argument will reach and the parts that each argument will not reach. This is how you show that you tested more than one part of your key procedure.

F. To complete part iii, you will write 1 sentence to identify the result of each call.

1. In the first rectangle, you will explain the result of the first call described in part i.

2. In the second rectangle, you will explain the result of the second call described in part i.

3. In each part be sure to:

i. Explain what happens in your program after each call completes.

ii. Connect to the purpose of your program.

Prompt 3d is worth 1 point out of 6 possible points for the Create Performance Task. These points come from each of your responses to parts i, ii, and iii in Prompt 3d. All written responses from this prompt refer to the key procedure code segments shared in Prompt 3c.

IV. SELF-ASSESSMENT

A. When you view your code segments and read your final written responses to Prompt 3d, be sure you are able to answer "yes" to each of the following questions. If not, revise your response to maximize your score. These are the questions that graders will ask themselves when they read your response to decide whether you should earn full credit for your response.

Question	Yes	No
1. Are all of your responses to Prompt 3d about testing the key procedure you wrote about in Prompt 3c?		
2. Look at the two calls you described in part i. ▸ For each call, do you name the procedure and name the argument? ▸ Is the first call's argument different from that of the second call? ▸ Does the first call reach a different segment of code than the second call?		
3. Look at your written response in part ii. Then answer the following questions about this part of your written response. ▸ Do you explain the condition(s) being tested by the first call to the procedure? ▸ Do you explain the condition(s) being tested by the second call to the procedure? ▸ Did you verify that the first call and second call reach different parts of the algorithm because of the different arguments used by each call?		
4. Look at your written response in part iii. Then answer the following questions about this part of your written response. ▸ Do you identify what happens in the program as a result of the first call? ▸ Do you identify what happens in the program as a result of the second call?		

Congratulations! Prompt 3d is the fourth and final prompt of your written responses to the Create Task. Save the document you created to hold your responses to parts i, ii, iii, and iv someplace safe and move on to Chapter 11.

Submitting Your Create Task to the Digital Portfolio

11

I. OVERVIEW

A. This chapter focuses on the final steps for submitting your Create Performance Task.

B. To submit your task you will need:

1. your program code document

2. your video

3. your written response images and files

C. You must submit this task to the Digital Portfolio by April 30.

II. STEPS TO PREPARE YOUR CREATE TASK FOR SUBMISSION

Test Tip

Open up the folder that you have been using to store all of these items. Now is when the file structure we set up at the start of this project will really help us to find what we need to submit this task. If you have been maintaining this structure, you can skip steps 1–3 here because you have finished these parts!

STEP 1: Create a PDF to hold all of your program code and image citations.

    i. Be organized with this PDF.

    ii. Several details to support you in creating this PDF are provided in Chapter 5.

STEP 2: Create a video to show your code running the program as described in your written response.

    i. The video must be less than 1 minute and under 30 MB.

    ii. The video must be saved with one of the following file extensions: .mp4, .wmv, .avi, or .mov.

    iii. Several details to support you in creating this PDF are provided in Chapter 6.

STEP 3: Prepare images and written responses to Prompts 3a, 3b, 3c, and 3d.

    i. Prompt 3a should consist of three written responses. Chapter 7 is focused on how to prepare these responses.

    ii. Prompt 3b should consist of two image files and three written responses. Chapter 8 provides more detail on this prompt.

    iii. Prompt 3c requires two image files and two written responses. Chapter 9 was created to support you with this part of the task.

    iv. Prompt 3d requires six written responses. Chapter 10 is focused on supporting you for this prompt.

STEP 4: Check the full task against the Create Checklist in Appendix D.

STEP 5: Communicate to the person who set up your Digital Portfolio access so this person knows that you plan to submit your Create Performance Task. This person is most likely your teacher.

STEP 6: Go to *https://digitalportfolio.collegeboard.org* and log in.

STEP 7: Find your class and click on "Create Performance Task."

STEP 8: Follow directions to upload the PDF of all of your Program Code.

    i. Hit the Final Submit button.

    ii. The site will prompt you to check the version you are uploading.

    iii. You will need to view this submission to verify that this is the correct version.

    iv. If this version is the correct version, confirm that you want to submit it. If not, you will need to upload a new version.

STEP 9: Follow directions to upload the video showing your program running.

    i. You will go through the same steps detailed above.

    ii. The system will not allow you to upload a video that is longer than 1 minute or larger than 30 MB.

STEP 10: Follow directions to upload the written responses.

    i. The site will prompt you to upload each part of the written responses separately.

    ii. At the time this book was created, this system was not available.

    iii. Be sure to read the directions carefully on the Digital Portfolio site for more information.

You are done with your Create Task! Celebrate! You have just handed in what will become 30% of your AP® score for AP® Computer Science Principles. Take a moment to reflect on all that you have learned.

PART II

THE END-OF-COURSE EXAM

Overview of the End-of-Course Exam

KEY DETAILS

A. As you prepare for your AP® Computer Science Principles (AP® CS Principles) End-of-Course Exam, keep the following details in mind:

1. The exam is administered in May during the AP® exam administration window.

2. The exam is 2 hours long and worth 70 percent of your AP® CS Principles score.

3. The End-of-Course Exam contains 70 multiple-choice questions (which allows a little over one-and-a-half minutes to answer each question).

4. There are three types of multiple-choice questions:

   i.   Single-Select Multiple-Choice

      ‣ There is one correct answer out of four possibilities (A–D).

      ‣ 57 out of the 70 multiple-choice exam questions follow this format.

   ii. Reading Passage Multiple-Choice

      ‣ One reading passage serves as a prompt for single-select multiple-choice questions.

      ‣ There are 5 questions on the End-of-Course Exam with this format.

iii. Multiple-Select Multiple-Choice

▸ There are two correct answers out of four possibilities (A–D).

▸ You need to choose both correct answers to get credit.

▸ There are 8 questions on the End-of-Course Exam with this format.

5. There is no penalty for guessing.

 Be sure you know when and where you will be taking the End-of-Course Exam. Check with your AP® teacher.

II. KEY CONCEPTS ON THE EXAM

A. The End-of-Course Exam will have questions on the following concepts. Included in the chart is an estimate of the number of questions you can expect for each concept.

Concept (Big Idea)	Percentage of Multiple-Choice Questions that will be about this Big Idea	Approximate Number of Multiple-Choice Questions (out of 70) that will be about this Big Idea	Chapter in *Crash Course* where topic is explained
Creative Development	10%–13%	7–9 questions	Chapter 14
Data	17%–22%	12–15 questions	Chapter 15
Algorithms and Programming	30%–35%	21–25 questions	Chapter 16
Computer Systems & Networks	11%–15%	8–11 questions	Chapter 17
Impact of Computing	21%–26%	15–18 questions	Chapter 18

III. **LANGUAGES AND INSTRUCTIONS ON THE EXAM**

A. There are two types of coding styles you will see on the exam:

1. block

2. text

B. Programming instructions will use one of the following four data types:

1. numbers

2. Booleans

3. strings

4. lists

IV. **SOME TIPS TO MAXIMIZE YOUR SCORE ON THE END-OF-COURSE EXAM**

A. The best way to prepare for many of the questions on the exam is to plan, write, and debug code.

1. Programming language ideas are provided in Chapter 2.

2. When you plan, be detailed in your design. Consider the inputs and outputs to every major decision made by your program.

3. When you code, name your variables and procedures with words that convey what the variables and procedures are doing for the code.

4. When you debug, do not stop at making the code work, but go further.

   i. Understand why it works.

   ii. Help someone else to understand why it works.

   iii. By doing so, you will understand coding well.

> *Helping others with their learning is not only a great way to learn how to code, but it also helps you learn how other people think about problems in a different way. This will not only help you to be better prepared to trace code for your End-of-Course Exam, but it will also make you a better problem solver.*

B. The End-of-Course Exam "language" is not a programming language.

    1. The coding style for questions is like pseudocode. It should make sense regardless of the language you normally use to code.

    2. You should be familiar with the syntax and other slight differences that you will see in questions written using this coding style.

> *It is important to do practice questions to get used to the coding style you will see on the End-of-Course Exam. There are some list indexes and styles that may surprise you, depending on the language you normally use. For example, the first element of a list is located at index 1 on the exam.*

C. Keep in mind that not all of the questions on the End-of-Course Exam relate to programming.

    1. There are questions that require you to read about computing innovations and consider all of the following about those innovations:

       i.   beneficial effects

       ii. harmful effects

       iii. unintended effects

       iv. data consumed, produced, and transformed

2. There are questions about data sets, data displays, and conclusions you can (or cannot) reach about the subject of these sets.

3. There are questions about computer systems and networking calculations as well as computing vocabulary.

D. This *Crash Course* gives you the tools you need to prepare for the End-of-Course Exam.

1. Read Chapter 13 to be sure you practice the coding style you will see in the End-of-Course Exam.

2. Use Chapter 14, in addition to programming and completing the Create Task, to prepare for questions that are about Creative Development.

3. Read Chapter 15 to be sure you are prepared for questions about Data.

4. Use Chapter 16, in addition to programming and completing the Create Task, to prepare for questions that are about Algorithms & Programming.

5. Read Chapter 17 to prepare for the vocabulary and calculations you need to be prepared to handle questions about Computer Systems & Networks.

6. Use Chapter 18, in addition to reading articles about innovative ideas, to prepare for the questions focused on the Impact of Computing.

7. Finally, you need to practice the multiple-choice questions.

   i. There is a code in the inside cover of your *Crash Course* that you can use to access a full-length End-of-Course Exam.

   ii. Chapter 19 of this book provides 25 more sample questions.

   iii. There are online resources provided at AP® Central, such as the questions in the back of the *Course and Exam Description*, to check your understanding.

iv. Ask your teacher to provide you with access to AP®
Classroom, which contains approximately 150 multiple-
choice questions.

*For your reference, the Exam Reference Sheet is provided
in Appendix E of this* Crash Course. *You should become
comfortable using this sheet, which will be provided to you for
the exam. This sheet contains instructions and explanations to
help you understand what the exam code will look like. Refer
to this sheet often when you do practice questions.*

Practicing the Multiple-Choice Programming Language

PSEUDOCODE USED ON THE EXAM

A. As you read this chapter, keep the following in mind:

1. The programming language you used to understand concepts may look slightly different from the pseudocode used on the AP® CS Principles Exam.

2. To be prepared for this exam, you should have practiced programming using one or more languages that have all of the following:

    i. A way to assign, display, and input variables.

    ii. The ability to use arithmetic operators such as addition, subtraction, multiplication, division, and modulus.

    iii. Procedures (also called functions or methods) that you can create or modify to take arguments (as inputs), perform an action, and/or return values (as outputs).

    iv. A way to compare two values as being equal or unequal (including greater than or less than).

    v. Boolean variables that can be created or used in statements to make decisions.

    vi. Conditional statements such as *if, else-if,* and *else.*

    vii. Iteration (loops such as a *for* loop or a *while* loop).

    viii. Lists and list operations (such as how to get an item into a list or how to add or remove items from a list).

    ix. A way to control how an element (such as a sprite, a pixel, a robot, or a character in a game) is moved.

THE EXAM REFERENCE SHEET

A. When you take your exam, you will get an Exam Reference Sheet.

1. This sheet summarizes the Programming Language you will see in the multiple-choice questions.

2. The Exam Reference Sheet was designed so all test-takers have a common reference for the following:

   i. Two types of programming languages:
      ▸ block
      ▸ text

   ii. Ways to do the following things in those languages:
      ▸ perform calculations
      ▸ handle and analyze logic
      ▸ store and manipulate information in variables and lists
      ▸ evaluate the order, conditions, and looping in code
      ▸ use code to create two-dimensional movements on a screen

B. The Exam Reference Sheet is organized by the following Categories of Instruction:

1. Assignment, Display, and Input

2. Arithmetic Operators and Numeric Procedures

3. Relational and Boolean Operators

4. Selection

5. Iteration

6. List Operations

7. Procedures and Procedure Calls

8. Robot

C. You should be familiar with most, if not all, of these categories no matter which language or environment you chose for this course.

III. CATEGORIES OF PROGRAMMING INSTRUCTIONS

Test Tip *Now is a good time to become familiar with the Exam Reference Sheet that will be provided to you when you take your exam. It is reproduced in Appendix E of this book.*

A. Category 1: Assignment, Display, or Input

1. In computer science, there are instructions that allow you to modify (assign), see (display), or get from a user (input) in a program.

2. Here are what these instructions will look like in a multiple-choice question:

How this would be used in code on the exam:	Instruction written in Text Coding Language	Instruction written in Block Coding Language
Assigns expression to a variable a.	a ← expression	a ← expression
Show the value of "expression" always followed by a space.	DISPLAY(expression)	DISPLAY expression
Accepts a value from a user and returns it.	INPUT()	INPUT

Note: The following multiple-choice questions are designed to help you practice the nuances of this code. Note the following before you try them:

▸ In actual multiple-choice questions, categories are often combined to check what you know about computer science.

▸ The examples provided here are to help you understand the syntax of the language you will see on the exam.

EXAMPLE 1:

Refer to the code shown at right. Suppose a person wants to test this code. When the code reaches line 2, the person types 7. What happens next?

```
Line 1: x ← 0
Line 2: y ← INPUT()
Line 3: DISPLAY(x)
Line 4: DISPLAY(y)
```

(A) A syntax error occurs. The program would not run. The INPUT() function requires a parameter.

(B) A logical error occurs. A person could use the INPUT() function in this way, but the assignment would not happen since nothing is returned from INPUT().

(C) The following output occurs: 0 7

(D) The following output occurs: 07

Answer: (C)

Choice (C) is correct. DISPLAY(expression) adds a space after printing expression. Choice (A) is not correct because INPUT() does exist and was called correctly as shown in the table. INPUT() does not require a parameter. If Line 2 said: "INPUT()← y", this would be an example of a syntax error since assignment happens from right to left. Choice (B) is not correct because INPUT()does accept and return whatever the user of the program types. Choice (D) is not correct because DISPLAY(expression) puts a space after printing.

EXAMPLE 2: TRUE OR FALSE

The following code is equivalent to the code in Example 1.

Line 1: $\boxed{x \leftarrow 0}$

Line 2: $\boxed{x \leftarrow \boxed{\text{INPUT}}}$

Line 3: $\boxed{\text{DISPLAY} \boxed{x}}$

Line 4: $\boxed{\text{DISPLAY} \boxed{y}}$

Answer: TRUE

Either blocks or text could be used for this exam. You need to be familiar with reading both types.

Test Tip

Notice how Example 2 refers back to the code in Example 1. It is common on the AP® CS Principles exam to have groups of questions that refer back to one situation. Thus, it is in your best interest to go through the exam in order and not skip around too much. Many questions will refer back to one set of code or a specific scenario. If you skip around, this can get confusing. You can always go back to check your answers, if you have extra time after you finish.

EXAMPLE 3 (SNEAK PEEK):

A person is writing their first program. They want the program to say "hello" to them. Here is pseudocode for what they hope the program will do:

1. Display "Please type your name."

2. The person types their name: *Bella*.

3. The computer will display: "Hello Bella".

Which of the following programs will behave as intended?

(A) x ← INPUT()
    DISPLAY("Hello")
    DISPLAY(x)
    DISPLAY("Please type your name.")

(B) DISPLAY("Please type your name.")
    x ← INPUT()
    DISPLAY("Hello")
    DISPLAY(x)

(C) DISPLAY("Hello")
    x ← INPUT()
    DISPLAY(x)
    DISPLAY("Please type your name.")

(D) x ← DISPLAY("Please type your name.")
    DISPLAY("Hello")
    DISPLAY(x)

Answer: (B)

This question is checking that you understand that order (sequence) of code matters and that the INPUT() command is needed to get user input in a program for this language. The space will print after "Hello" since this happens by default through the call to the DISPLAY instruction. Choice (A) is incorrect because the input command is called before prompting the user. Choice (C) is incorrect because "Please type your name" should be the first call to DISPLAY. Choice (D) would be a syntax error since DISPLAY does not return anything.

Test Tip

The example questions included in this chapter will help you learn the Exam Reference Sheet. Notice that Example 3 is labeled "(Sneak Peek)." This means that Example 3 is a multiple-choice question similar to what you will see on your exam. Example 2 (which shows no label) is included so you can check your understanding of the reference and/or practice code that you might see on the exam. There are no TRUE/ FALSE questions on the End-of-Course Exam.

B. Category 2: Arithmetic Operators and Numeric Procedures

1. These are instructions that allow you to turn two inputs into one output. All of these, the two inputs and the output, are the same data type.

2. An example of an operator is addition. Notice that 2 + 3 equals 5. The inputs are 2 and 3, the output is 5, and all of these are numbers.

3. This category could be seen in code in combination with any of the other categories in a multiple-choice question.

How this would be used on the exam:	Instruction in Text or Block Language	Example of what this operation does	
Perform addition on two values a and b. Note: + is also a String concatenation operator.	a+b	a ← 3 b ← 2 DISPLAY(a+b)	a ← 3 b ← 2 DISPLAY (a+b)
		The output: 5	
Perform subtraction on two values a and b.	a-b	a ← 3 b ← 2 DISPLAY(a-b)	a ← 3 b ← 2 DISPLAY (a-b)
		The output: 1	
Perform multiplication on two values a and b.	a*b	a ← 3 b ← 2 DISPLAY(a*b)	a ← 3 b ← 2 DISPLAY (a*b)
		The output: 6	

(continued)

How this would be used on the exam:	Instruction in Text or Block Language	Example of what this operation does	
Perform division on two values a and b.	a/b	a ← 3 b ← 2 DISPLAY(a/b)	a ← 3 b ← 2 DISPLAY (a/b)
		The output: 1.5	
Find the remainder (modulus) when a is divided by b.	a MOD b	a ← 17 b ← 5 DISPLAY(a MOD b)	a ← 17 b ← 5 DISPLAY (a MOD b)
		The output: 2	
Find a random number from a to b, including a and b.	Text: RANDOM(a,b) Block: RANDOM a,b	a ← 1 b ← 3 RANDOM(a,b)	a ← 1 b ← 3 RANDOM a,b
		The output: 1, 2, or 3	

Test Tip

Both text and block languages are shown next to each other here and on the Exam Reference Sheet. On the End-of-Course Exam, a question would use one language or the other, never both.

4. Some tips about MODULUS (MOD):

    i. Most of the operations above are not new to you. However, modulus may be a new idea. Here are some tips to help you understand this operation:

▸ The modulus of two numbers is the remainder of these two numbers being divided.

– Here are some examples of modulus in action:

10 MOD 1=0 (there is no remainder since 1 divides evenly into 10)

10 MOD 2=0

10 MOD 3=1

10 MOD 4=2 (4 divides evenly into 10 twice with a remainder of 2)

10 MOD 6=4 (6 divides evenly into 10 once, remainder is 4)

▸ Here are some "rules" about modulus:

– Any modulus calculation can be understood using long division until it becomes automatic for you.

$$\begin{array}{r} 7 \\ 3\overline{)22} \\ -21 \\ \hline 1 \end{array}$$

a. Example: 22 MOD 3 is the remainder of 22 divided by 3 is shown to the right. (remainder is 1)

b. So 22 MOD 3 = 1

– If the number to the left of MOD is a multiple of the number to the right of MOD, the result is 0:

a. Example: 20 MOD 4 is 0 since 20 is a multiple of 4

– If the number to the left of MOD is less than the number to the right of MOD, the result is the number to the left of MOD:

$$\begin{array}{r} 0 \\ 20\overline{)4} \\ -0 \\ \hline 4 \end{array}$$

a. Example: 4 MOD 20 is 4 since 20 is too large to go into 4. See long division to the right. (remainder is 4)

– You cannot have 0 to the right of the MOD

a. Example: 20 MOD 0 does not make sense since this would be like dividing by 0

- You can have 0 to the left of the MOD

    a. Example: 0 MOD 4 is 0 since 0 divided by any number that is not 0 is 0 with a remainder of 0.

> *Watch for division by 0 errors in MOD calculations—this can get a little confusing. 20 MOD 0 is not valid. 0 MOD 20 is 0. The 0 cannot be to the right of MOD.*

▸ Modulus is often used in a program for the following purposes:

- To determine if numbers are even or odd.

    a. If 2 is to the right of MOD, the result of this operation will tell you if the number to the left of MOD is even or odd.

        • Example: 7 MOD 2 is 1. This means 7 is odd.

        • Example: 8 MOD 2 is 0. This means 8 is even.

    b. General Rule:

       If x MOD 2 is 1, x is ODD.

       If x MOD 2 is 0, x is EVEN.

- To cause periodic behavior such as going back to the start of a list.

    a. Suppose you have a list that has a certain number of items. To prevent going beyond the end of the list, modulus can be used.

    b. If i is the index number and a list with 10 items is called aList, you can use modulus to prevent going beyond the end of the list as i increases. Do this by calling each element of the list as follows: aList[i MOD 10].

– To convert between number systems.

   a. Suppose you want to convert 1600 hours (military time) to our normal AM/PM clock time. 1600 hours is 16:00. The "normal" clock time is a 12-hour system. Applying a modulus of 12 will do the trick!

   b. 16 MOD 12 is 4. 16:00 in military time is 4:00.

   c. If you research *MODULUS* online, you might see it referred to as "clock time" for this reason.

EXAMPLE 4 (SNEAK PEEK):

A teacher is organizing students into 5 groups. As students enter the room, they are assigned a number, 1, 2, 3, 4, or 5, to indicate their group number. The 6th student to enter the room should be assigned group number 1. A programmer is writing a procedure to simulate this system. The procedure is called assignGroup(studentCount). It uses studentCount, a parameter that is incremented each time a new student enters the room, as an input and returns the correct group number that the student will be assigned.

Which of the following code segments is a correct implementation of assignGroup(studentCount)?

```
(A) PROCEDURE assignGroup(studentCount)
    {
        RETURN(studentCount MOD 5)
    }
```

```
(B) PROCEDURE assignGroup(studentCount)
    {
        IF (studentCount MOD 5 == 0)
          RETURN 5
        ELSE
          RETURN(studentCount MOD 5)
    }
```

(C) PROCEDURE assignGroup(studentCount)
```
{
    RETURN(studentCount MOD 5 + 1)
}
```

(D) PROCEDURE assignGroup(studentCount)
```
{
    RETURN(studentCount / 5 + 1)
}
```

Answer: (B)

Consider different values of studentCount. If studentCount is 1, then the return should be 1. That would happen in the procedures written for (A) and (B). So, the solution cannot be (C) or (D). Indeed, (A) and (B) would work for studentCount values of 1, 2, 3, and 4. At 5, (A) does not work. 5 MOD 5 is 0. The 5th student should be assigned group 5 so the return should be 5. (B) handles this situation correctly. Note that (B) would continue to work for higher studentCount values. When studentCount is 6, 6 MOD 5 is 1, correctly assigning group number 1. At 10, again, (B) would handle the situation correctly by assigning group 5 to the 10th student.

EXAMPLE 5:

What would be displayed when the code in line 6–13 are reached?

```
Line 1: w ← 0
Line 2: x ← 4
Line 3: y ← 5
Line 4: z ← 0
Line 5: w ← x*y
Line 6: DISPLAY(z-x*y)
Line 7: DISPLAY(z-w)
Line 8: DISPLAY(y/x)
Line 9: DISPLAY(y MOD x)
Line 10: DISPLAY(x MOD y)
Line 11: DISPLAY(w MOD x)
Line 12: DISPLAY(z MOD x)
Line 13: DISPLAY(x MOD z)
```

Answers:

Line 6: –20 The order of operations is followed.

Line 7: –20 Since *w* was assigned *x*y*, Lines 6 and 7 are logically equivalent.

Line 8: 1.25 Division is performed.

> *Notice that even though the variables* y *and* x *are integers, the multiple-choice exam division operator output is a quotient. The data type widens. This may be different from the language you are using.*

Line 9: 1 The remainder of 5/4 is 1 since 4 goes into 5 with a remainder of 1.

Line 10: 4 The remainder of 4/5 is 4 since 5 does not go into 4. In general, if the positive number to the left of MOD is smaller than the number to the right, the result is the number to the left of the MOD. So for example, 4 MOD 6 is 4, 2 MOD 7 is 2, 8 MOD 10 is 8.

Line 11: 0 The remainder of 20/4 is 0 since the result of the division is 5 with no remainder.

Line 12: 0 See explanation for Line 10 and Line 11—this is an example of both.

Line 13: This is an error. 0 to the right of MOD is invalid since you cannot divide by 0.

C. Category 3: Relational and Boolean Operators

1. A Boolean is a special data type that has one of two values: `true` or `false`.

2. A Boolean may be returned

    i.   as a result of evaluating a condition,

    ii. as a result of comparing two values, or

    iii. when evaluating one or more Boolean conditions.

3. This category could be seen in code in combination with any of the other categories in a multiple-choice question.

How this would be used on the exam:	Instruction in Text or Block Language	Example of what this operation does	
Compares values stored in a and b. Returns true if the statement is true; false otherwise.	a = b a ≠ b a > b a < b a ≥ b a ≤ b	a ← 3 b ← 2 DISPLAY(a>b)	a ← 3 b ← 3 DISPLAY a > b
		The output: true	
Evaluates to true if condition is false; otherwise evaluates to true. You can look at NOT as the instruction that changes true to false and false to true.	Text: NOT condition Block: NOT condition	a ← 3 b ← NOT(a=3) DISPLAY(b)	a ← 3 b ← NOT a = 3 DISPLAY b
		The output: false	
Evaluates to true if condition1 and condition2 are true; otherwise evaluates to false.	Text: condition1 AND condition2 Block: condition1 AND condition2	a ← false b ← true c ← a AND b DISPLAY(c)	a ← false b ← true c ← a AND b DISPLAY c
		The output: false	
Evaluates to true if condition1 or condition2 are true; otherwise evaluates to false.	Text: condition1 OR condition2 Block: condition1 OR condition2	a ← true b ← false c ← a OR b DISPLAY(c)	a ← true b ← false c ← a OR b DISPLAY c
		The output: true	

4. Using Truth Tables to Analyze Boolean Logic

   i. A truth table is useful to understand Boolean expressions.

  ii. Here are truth tables to help you understand AND, OR, and NOT in a bit more detail.

 iii. NOT is a Boolean operation.

> ▸ Let's use a truth table to study the possibilities for the Boolean expression: NOT(A), where A is a Boolean variable.

> ▸ To do this, start by filling in the left column with the possible values A could have—true or false.

A	NOT(A)
true	false
false	true

> ▸ Then, fill in the right column with the result of the NOT(A) operation. Since NOT means "opposite of," NOT(true) is false and NOT(false) is true.

 iv. AND is a Boolean operation.

> ▸ To the right, see the truth table that shows the possibilities for the Boolean expression A AND B, where A and B are both Boolean variables.

A	B	A AND B
true	true	true
true	false	false
false	true	false
false	false	false

> ▸ To do this on your own, start by filling in the left two columns with the possible values A and B could have.

> ▸ Because there are two Booleans (A and B) there are $2^2 = 4$ possible outcomes for A and B, combined. That is why there are four rows.

> ▸ Note that A AND B will only return true if both A and B are true. Otherwise, A AND B returns false.

v. OR is also a binary Boolean operation.

▸ Above, see the truth table (on the right) created to analyze the possibilities for the Boolean expression A OR B.

A	B	A OR B
true	true	true
true	false	true
false	true	true
false	false	false

▸ Note that A OR B will only return false if both A and B are false. Otherwise, A OR B returns true.

When you are looking at a Boolean expression, true OR *"anything" always returns* true. false AND *"anything" always returns* false, *where* "anything" *could be any boolean expression. This is called short-circuiting. Recognizing this pattern will save time on multiple-choice questions.*

5. Tips (and vocabulary) about Boolean Operators

i. Applying NOT to Conditions.

▸ When applying NOT to relational operators, be careful. The opposite of an inequality can be misleading. Specifically, see the following list:

NOT(NOT a) is a.
NOT(a<b) is a≥b.
NOT(a>b) is a≤b.
NOT(a=b) is a≠b.
NOT(a≠b) is a=b.
NOT(a≥b) is a<b.
NOT(a≤b) is a>b.

▸ When applying NOT to statements with AND or OR, the following rules can be used. These are commonly called DeMorgan's Laws.

NOT (A AND B) is NOT A OR NOT B
NOT (A OR B) is NOT A AND NOT B

- Even though you do not need to know these laws by name, you do need to know how to apply them to conditions in code.

- These laws will save you time when you are looking at code.

Truth tables are a tool used for logical proofs in Boolean Algebra. They are not the same as a geometry proof, but they will be a handy tool to help you understand or plan code. You would never be asked to do a truth table on the End-of-Course Exam, but using them to think through logic can save time.

EXAMPLE 6: USE TRUTH TABLES TO PROVE DEMORGAN'S LAWS:

A: Here is a proof of the first law: NOT(A AND B) is <u>NOT(A) OR NOT(B)</u>

A	B	A AND B	NOT (A AND B)	NOT A	NOT B	NOT(A)OR NOT(B)
true	true	true	false	false	false	false
true	false	false	true	false	true	true
false	true	false	true	true	false	true
false	false	false	true	true	true	true

1. To work this out on paper, start with the column titles and the first two columns filled in with the four possibilities for A and B.

2. Then fill in the table, one column at a time, from left to right.

3. Each column will use one or two columns before it. For example, notice how the column titled, "NOT(A AND B)" depends on the one to its left, "A AND B".

Now, notice the last column titled, "NOT(A) OR NOT(B)". Can you see how that column has the same values as the column titled, "NOT(A AND B)"? This means that NOT(A AND B) is equivalent to <u>NOT(A) OR NOT(B)</u>.

Test Tip

Try the second proof out on your own to practice truth tables. Then, check your understanding by looking at the solution.

B: Here is a proof of the second law: NOT(A OR B) is <u>NOT(A) AND NOT(B)</u>

A	B	A OR B	NOT(A OR B)	NOT A	NOT B	NOT A AND NOT B
true	true	true	false	false	false	false
true	false	true	false	false	true	false
false	true	true	false	true	false	false
false	false	false	true	true	true	true

Now, notice the last column titled, "NOT(A) AND NOT(B)". Can you see how that column has the same values as the column titled, "NOT(A OR B)"? This means that NOT(A OR B) is equivalent to <u>NOT A AND NOT B.</u>

EXAMPLE 7(SNEAK PEEK):

In the following statement, value1, value2, and result are Boolean variables.

> result ← NOT(value1) AND value2

Which of the following statements is equivalent to the statement above for all possible values of statem1 and statem2?

(A) result ← NOT(value1 OR NOT(value2))

(B) result ← NOT(value1) OR NOT(value2)

(C) result ← NOT(value1 AND NOT(value2))

(D) result ← NOT(value1 OR value2)

Answer: (A)

Choice (A) is correct because, by applying the second DeMorgan's Law, NOT(value1 OR NOT (value2)) is equivalent to NOT(value1) AND NOT(NOT(value2)) and simplifying, we arrive at the original expression:

$$NOT(value1) \text{ AND } NOT(NOT(value2)) =$$
$$NOT(value1) \text{ AND } value2$$

Looking at Choice (B), you can see that it is not equivalent without simplying. We can simplify Choice (C) using the first law: NOT(value1 AND NOT (value2)) = NOT(value1) OR NOT(NOT(value2))= NOT(value1) OR value2. This is different from the original statement since there is an "OR" rather than an "AND". We can do the same with Choice (D), using the second law: NOT(value1 OR value2) = NOT(value1) AND NOT(value2). This is different from the original statement since both value1 and value2 have a NOT in front of them.

Test Tip

There are two types of multiple-choice questions on the End-of-Course Exam: Single-Select Multiple-Choice and Multiple-Select Multiple-Choice. Example 8 shown below is an example of a Multiple-Select Multiple-Choice question for which there are two correct answers. The exam lists these types of questions separately from the other types of multiple-choice questions and specifies that two answers are correct. No partial credit is awarded. You need to choose both correct answers in order to earn credit for the question.

EXAMPLE 8 (SNEAK PEEK):

In the following statement, x, y, and result are Boolean variables.

result ← NOT(x) AND y

Which of the following statements produce the same result as the statement above for all possible values of x and y?

Select <u>two</u> answers.

```
(A) result ← true           (B) result ← true
    IF (NOT (x))                IF (x)
        IF (y)                     result ← false
            result ← false      ELSE
                                   IF (NOT(y))
                                       result ← false
```

```
(C) result ← false          (D) result ← false
    IF (NOT (x))                IF (x)
        IF (y)                     result ← true
            result ← true       ELSE
                                   IF (NOT(y))
                                       result ← true
```

Answer: (B), (C)

You can analyze this using a truth table.

x	y	NOT(x)	NOT(y)	NOT(x) AND y
true	true	false	false	false
true	false	false	true	false
false	true	true	false	true
false	false	true	true	false

Notice that the circled part indicates that the statement NOT(x) AND y will only be true if x is false and y is true. If x is true to start, the statement NOT(x) AND y will be false. If both x and y are false, the result will be false.

Choice (A) is not correct because this code would set result to false IF NOT(x) AND y were true. Choice (D) is not correct because this code would set result to true IF (x) OR NOT(y) were true. Both (A) and (D) are different from the original statement. Choice (B) is correct and it is easiest to see this using DeMorgan's Laws. The code written in (B) says that result if false IF(x) OR NOT(y) are false. So it would be true if NOT(x or NOT(y)), which is equivalent to NOT(x) AND y, the original statement. Choice (C) is correct because the code would set result to true IF (y) AND NOT(x) were true. (B) and (C) are logically equivalent to the original statement.

Test Tip

Example 8 (Sneak Peek) gives you an idea of the type of question you should be able to handle on the End-of-Course Exam. For more End-of-Course Exam examples, see Chapter 19 and be sure to check out the College Board's AP® CS Principles Course and Exam Description on the AP® Central website as well as the full-length online exam available with this Crash Course book.

D. Category 4: Selection

1. Selection is one of the three major components of any algorithm in computer science. The other two components are sequencing (order) and iteration (looping).

2. In an algorithm, selection is used for the following situations:

   i.   You know what you want to do when a condition is true. This is often called an `IF`-statement.

   ii. You know what you want to do when a condition is false. This is often the `ELSE` in an `IF-ELSE` statement.

3. This is what *selection* instructions will look like in a multiple-choice question:

How this would be used on the exam:	Instruction in Text	Instruction in Block

The code in `<block of statements>` would be executed only if the Boolean expression `condition` is true; nothing would happen if condition is `false`	`IF(condition)`
	`{`
	`<block of statements>`
	`}`
		IF condition
		
		block of statements

(continued)

How this would be used on the exam:	Instruction in Text	Instruction in Block

The code in <first block of statements> is executed if condition is true; otherwise the code in <second block of statements> is executed	IF(condition)
	{
	<first block of statements>
	}
	ELSE
	{
	<second block of statements>
	}
		IF condition
		
		first block of statements
		
		ELSE
		
		second block of statements

EXAMPLE 9 (SNEAK PEEK):

Consider the code segment below.

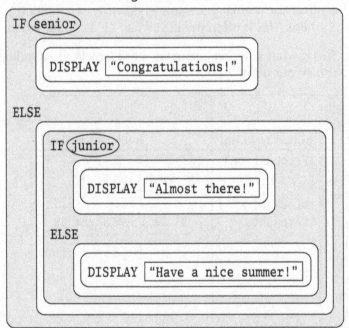

If the variable `junior` is false, what is displayed?

(A) "Have a nice summer!"

(B) "Congratulations!"

(C) Both A and B

(D) It is impossible to determine.

Answer: (D)

Information about whether the Boolean variable `senior` is true or not is not included. If `senior` is `true`, then "Congratulations!" would display. If not, only "Have a nice summer!" would display.

E. Category 5: Iteration

1. Iteration is one of the three major components of any algorithm in computer science. The other two components are sequencing (order) and selection (using *if* statements or *if-else* statements to choose which block of statements will execute).

2. In an algorithm, iteration is used when you would like to repeat a behavior. Some examples include:

   i. You want to do something a certain number of times.

   ii. You want to do something until a condition is true.

   iii. You have a collection of data and you need to see each element in the collection.

3. This is what *iteration* will look like in a multiple-choice question:

How this would be used on the exam:	Instruction in Text	Instruction in Block
The code in `<block of statements>` would be executed n times	```REPEAT n TIMES { <block of statements> }```	```REPEAT n TIMES block of statements```
The code in `<block of statements>` would be executed until the Boolean expression condition is true	```REPEAT UNTIL (condition) { <block of statements> }```	```REPEAT until condition block of statements```
The variable `item` holds each element of list in order from first element to last element. The code in `<block of statements>` is executed once for each time `item` is assigned.	```FOR EACH item in list { <block of statements> }```	```FOR EACH item IN list block of statements```

EXAMPLE 10 (SNEAK PEEK):

Consider the following code segment.

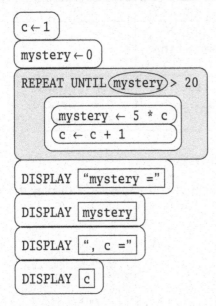

```
c ← 1
mystery ← 0
REPEAT UNTIL (mystery) > 20
    mystery ← 5 * c
    c ← c + 1

DISPLAY "mystery ="
DISPLAY mystery
DISPLAY ", c ="
DISPLAY c
```

What is displayed as a result of running the program code?

(A) mystery = 20, c = 5

(B) mystery = 25, c = 6

(C) mystery = 30, c = 6

(D) mystery = 25, c = 5

Answer: (B)

Tables can help in tracing loops. Before the loop, mystery is 0 and c is 1. The loop condition is not evaluated until the last block in the loop is processed.

Loop number	mystery > 20	mystery	c
Before First Loop	Loop has not happened yet	0	1
1	false (it is 0)	5	2
2	false (it is 5)	10	3

(continued)

Loop number	mystery > 20	mystery	c
3	false (it is 10)	15	4
4	false (it is 15)	20	5
5	false (it is 20, so not greater than 20)	25	6
6	true (it is 25)	Loop is broken; mystery and c will not change.	

EXAMPLE 11 (SNEAK PEEK):

Which of the following blocks of code does NOT display the same values as Example 10?

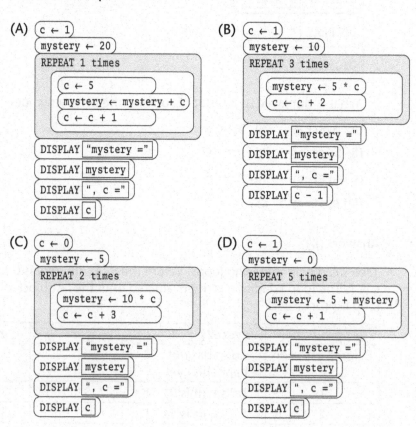

(A)
```
c ← 1
mystery ← 20
REPEAT 1 times
    c ← 5
    mystery ← mystery + c
    c ← c + 1
DISPLAY "mystery ="
DISPLAY mystery
DISPLAY ", c ="
DISPLAY c
```

(B)
```
c ← 1
mystery ← 10
REPEAT 3 times
    mystery ← 5 * c
    c ← c + 2
DISPLAY "mystery ="
DISPLAY mystery
DISPLAY ", c ="
DISPLAY c - 1
```

(C)
```
c ← 0
mystery ← 5
REPEAT 2 times
    mystery ← 10 * c
    c ← c + 3
DISPLAY "mystery ="
DISPLAY mystery
DISPLAY ", c ="
DISPLAY c
```

(D)
```
c ← 1
mystery ← 0
REPEAT 5 times
    mystery ← 5 + mystery
    c ← c + 1
DISPLAY "mystery ="
DISPLAY mystery
DISPLAY ", c ="
DISPLAY c
```

Answer: (C)

For all of these, remember that the goal was that the output is NOT "mystery = 25, c = 6".

Choice (C) would not display: mystery = 25, c = 6. Before the loop, c is assigned 0 and mystery is assigned 5. In the loop, mystery is assigned (in order): 0, 30 and c is assigned (in order): 3, 6. So, instead the display would be: mystery = 30, c = 6.

Choice (A) would display correctly. Before the loop, c is assigned 1 (it does not matter what this value is since it is reassigned in the loop). In the one loop, c is assigned 5, mystery is assigned 25, then c is incremented by 1 so it is assigned 6. At the time of the output, each variable has the correct value.

Tracing Choice (B) is more challenging. Before the loop, c is assigned 1 and mystery is assigned 10 (it does not matter what this value is since it is reassigned in the loop). In the loop, c is assigned (in order): 3, 5, 7 and mystery is assigned (in order, note that it depends on c for each iteration): 5, 15, 25. mystery will print correctly. c will appear correctly since the output following c is c - 1 so instead of printing 7, 6 will correctly print.

Choice (D) also requires tracing. Before the loop, c is assigned 1 and mystery is assigned 0. In the loop, c is assigned (in order): 2, 3, 4, 5, 6 and mystery is assigned (in order): 5,10,15,20,25. At the end of the loop, mystery is 25 and c is 6.

F. Category 6: List Operations

1. A list is a collection of items of the same type.

2. Lists are handled differently in each language. It is important to know the following:

   i. The way lists are created, modified, and accessed on the Exam Reference Sheet may have a different syntax than you practiced.

    ii. No matter the language, a common vocabulary is important:

- the list = the collection itself
- the index = the location in the list where an item is found
- the item = one element of the list

3. Key points you need to know about lists:

    i. An error is returned if you try to access an element that is outside of the list.

- The smallest list index is 1.
- The largest list index is the length of the list.

    ii. There are three ways you can add elements to a list:

- You can initialize from a list of values (assignment by list variable).
- You can add one element at a time at the end of the list (called APPEND).
- You can add one element at a time at a specific location in the list (called INSERT).

    iii. You can remove elements from the list by their location (called REMOVE).

    iv. When elements are added or removed the length of the list is automatically adjusted.

4. Details of list operations.

How this would be used on the exam:	Instruction in Text	Instruction in Block
Returns the element of aList at index i.	aList[i]	list i
Returns the first element of aList.	alist[1]	list 1

How this would be used on the exam:	Instruction in Text	Instruction in Block
Assigns a copy of bList to the list aList.	alist ← blist	alist ← blist
Assigns the value of aList[j] to aList[i]	alist[i] ← alist[j]	alist i ← alist j
Creates an empty list and assigns it to aList	aList ← []	alist ← ☐
Assigns v1, v2, and v3,... to aList[1], aList[2], and aList[3],... respectively.	alist ← [v1, v2, v3, ...]	list ← value1, value2, value3
The variable item holds each element of aList in order from first element to last element. The code in <block of statements> is executed once for each time item is assigned.	FOR EACH item in aList { <block of statements> }	FOR EACH item IN list block of statements
Inserts value into aList at location i. Shifts values in locations larger than i to the right. Increases length of list by 1.	INSERT(alist, i, value)	INSERT list, i, value
Place value at end of aList. Increase length of list by 1.	APPEND(aList, value)	APPEND list, value

(continued)

How this would be used on the exam:	Instruction in Text	Instruction in Block
Remove item at index i from aList and shifts any values at locations larger than i to the left. Reduces length of aList by 1.	REMOVE(aList, i)	REMOVE list, i
Returns the length of aList	LENGTH(aList)	LENGTH list

EXAMPLE 12 (SNEAK PEEK):

A retail company uses a database to store key statistics. The prices of all items in the store are stored in a list called prices indexed from 1 to n. The following code segment is intended to assign the index of the item that has the highest price to maxLoc. There is some missing code.

```
i ← 0
maxLoc ← 1
n ← LENGTH(prices)
REPEAT n times
{
   i ← i + 1
   <MISSING CODE>
}
```

Which of the following code segments can replace <MISSING CODE> so that the program works as intended?

```
(A) IF (prices[i] > maxLoc)
    {
       maxLoc ← prices[i]
    }
```

```
(B) IF (prices[i] > prices[maxLoc])
    {
       maxLoc ← i
    }
```

```
(C) IF (prices[i] < prices[maxLoc])
    {
      maxLoc ← i
    }
(D) IF (prices[i] > prices[maxLoc])
    {
      maxLoc ← prices[i]
    }
```

Answer: (B)

The question wants you to assign the index, not the element itself, to maxLoc. Choice (D) assigns the element to maxLoc. Choice (A) compares the value stored at i to maxLoc, which is not a value in the list. Choice (C) uses an incorrect inequality, but does correctly pass the index.

EXAMPLE 13:

A track coach is writing code to track the mile times of runners on the team over the year. The coach has an alphabetized list of each team member's name called namesList. When a new team member is added to the team, the coach wants to add this person to the list in the correct spot. Which list operation is probably NOT a part of this solution?

(A) APPEND

(B) INSERT

(C) REMOVE

(D) LENGTH

Answer: (C)

REMOVE removes elements of the list, which is not related to this problem. All other operations shown may be useful.

EXAMPLE 14 (SNEAK PEEK):

Consider the namesList from Example 13. The coach wants to write code to display all of the elements in namesList.

Which of the following code segments will NOT function as intended?

(A)
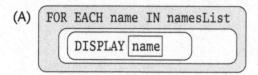

(B)
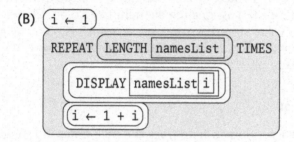

(C)
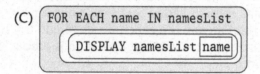

(D)
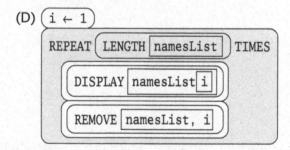

Answer: (C)

All of the other blocks display each element of the list. Choices (A) and (B) accomplish the same task, but Choice (A) uses a FOR EACH loop and Choice (B) uses a REPEAT loop. Notice how much easier it is to read Choice (A) rather than Choice (B), though they are equivalent. Choice (B) requires an extra variable not needed in Choice (A). Choice (D) would be a strange approach, since the list is empty at the end of this loop, but it does display each element before removing it. Choice (C) does not work correctly. Choice (C) would return an error since name is the name itself, not an index of namesList.

G. Category 7: Procedures

1. A procedure is a way to manage a group of instructions in a program.

2. Each language has its own unique way to create and use a procedure.

3. In the End-of-Course Exam, there are two types of procedures you will see:

   i.   a procedure that manages a group of instructions

   ii. a procedure that manages a group of instructions and returns a result

4. For either type of procedure:

   i.   You can have 0 or more parameters. It is possible that a procedure has no inputs (parameters).

   ii. To call the procedure without creating an error, include the name of the procedure and the correct number of parameters.

   iii. Do not worry about the data type.

   ▶ Whether they are numbers or strings, for example, will be specified in the question.

   ▶ Procedure definitions do not include the parameter data type, nor is the return data type specified.

5. What a PROCEDURE will look like on your exam:

How this would be used on the exam:	Instruction in Text	Instruction in Block
PROCEDURE tells the program to complete instructions. PROCEDURE will have a name and 0 or more inputs (parameters).	PROCEDURE name(parameter1, parameter2,...) { <instructions> }	PROCEDURE name │parameter1, parameter2,...│ (instructions)
PROCEDURE tells the program to complete instructions. PROCEDURE can have 0 or more inputs (parameters). This PROCEDURE is different since it returns the value of expression. The RETURN can appear anywhere in the PROCEDURE and causes a return from the PROCEDURE back to the program that called it.	PROCEDURE name(parameter1, parameter2,...) { <instructions> RETURN (expression) }	PROCEDURE name │parameter1, parameter2,...│ (instructions) RETURN │expression│

EXAMPLE 15 (SNEAK PEEK):

A person is writing a program that uses a list to track the number of minutes walked each day. The list is called minutesList. It is indexed from 1 to n. Each element represents the minutes walked on each day. For example, minutesList[1] would return the number of minutes the person walked on day 1.

This person wants to write a procedure called findAverage that should take a list with at least one element as a parameter and return the average of that list. The person intends to use this procedure to find the average of `minutesList`. However, there is an error in the code.

What is the error?

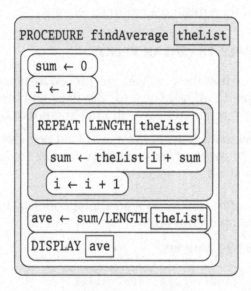

(A) There is no n, so the loop will not stop.

(B) `theList` is different from `minutesList` so this procedure would not work correctly for `minutesList`

(C) the following line has an error:

```
ave ← sum/LENGTH theList
```

(D) A return statement is missing

Answer: (D)

Choice (A) is incorrect since n is equal to the return from the call to `LENGTH`, which makes sense. Choice (B) is incorrect since this `PROCEDURE` would work with any list you use to call it. The call to this `PROCEDURE` would include `minutesList` as the parameter. Choice (C) might have been tempting if, when you looked at this you thought, "What if `theList` has no elements?" Notice that, in the directions, `findAverage` takes a list with "at least one element." So, possible division by 0 is controlled before the procedure is called. Choice (D) is correct because the procedure was described as returning a value. This is different from a DISPLAY command, which simply shows the value to the program user. The procedure is missing a return statement.

EXAMPLE 16 (SNEAK PEEK):

Suppose that the findAverage procedure works as described in Example 15 above. The error was fixed and the DISPLAY command has been replaced by a return statement that correctly returns ave.

Assume that minutesList has at least one element and you are trying to use the findAverage procedure to display the average of minutesList.

Which of the following is an appropriate way to call this procedure to accomplish this task?

Select <u>two</u> answers.

(A)

(B) DISPLAY findAverage minutesList

(C)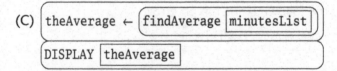

(D)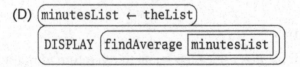

Correct Answers: (B), (C)

Choice (A) is not appropriate since the average would be returned, but not displayed. Choice (D) is not appropriate since theList may not exist. We are trying to find the average of minutesList, not theList. Choices (B) and (C) both correctly pass the parameter (minutesList) and display the output.

EXAMPLE 17 (SNEAK PEEK):

A person is creating a program to help with processing lists.

Consider the following procedure definitions:

Procedure Call	Explanation
isFound(theList, element)	Returns true if element is found in theList and returns false otherwise.
removeDuplicates(theList)	Returns a list that has no repeated elements. The element order does not change. So, if aList is {3,5,3,4}, removeDuplicates(aList) would return {3,5,4}.

The isFound procedure has already been created and tested. The programmer now wants to use isFound to create the removeDuplicates procedure.

Which of the following is NOT a correct procedure definition for removeDuplicates?

```
(A) PROCEDURE removeDuplicates(theList)
    {
      i ← 1
      newList ← []
      REPEAT LENGTH(theList) TIMES
      {
        IF (NOT(isFound(newList, theList[i])))
        {
          APPEND(newList, theList[i])
        }
        i ← i+1
      }
      RETURN (newList)
    }
```

```
(B) PROCEDURE removeDuplicates(theList)
    {
      newList ← []
      FOR EACH elem IN theList
      {
        IF (NOT(isFound(newList, elem)))
        {
          APPEND(newList, elem)
        }
      }
      RETURN (newList)
    }

(C) PROCEDURE removeDuplicates(theList)
    {
      i ← 1
      newList ← []
      n ← 1
      REPEAT LENGTH(theList) TIMES
      {
        IF (NOT(isFound(newList, theList[i])))
        {
          INSERT(newList, theList[i], n)
          n ← n+1
        }
        i ← i+1
      }
      RETURN (newList)
    }

(D) PROCEDURE removeDuplicates(theList)
    {
      newList ← []
      FOR EACH elem IN theList
      {
        IF (NOT(isFound(newList, theList[i])))
        {
          APPEND(newList, elem)
        }
      }
      RETURN (newList)
    }
```

Answer: (D)

Choices (A), (B), and (C) are all examples for how you can use valid FOR loops and list procedures to fill the newList with unique elements from theList. To use INSERT in Choice (C) you need two different indices, i and n, to keep track of where you are in theList and where you are in newList, respectively. Choice (B) shows you what a valid FOR EACH loop looks like in the End-of-Course Exam code. Choice (D) is incorrect because there is no i value in the code. The correct way to access elements in theList is to use elem. elem is the variable that is iterating through theList in this FOR EACH loop. Attempting to use i would be a syntax error.

H. Category 8: Robot

1. This category gives you a way to move around a two-dimensional grid.

2. With these types of questions, you can count on the following:

   i. The triangle is the robot.

      ‣ The triangle points in the direction the robot is facing.

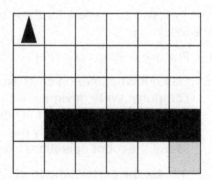

   ‣ The robot shown is in the top left corner and is facing up.

> ▸ The robot cannot make an "illegal" move. This means that it cannot go into the solid black squares or leave the grid.

   ii. The robot may or may not be moving in toward a goal.

> ▸ If the robot is moving toward a goal, this would be explained in the question.

> ▸ In addition, the goal would be indicated with a symbol (other than the triangle) to show you where the goal is located in the grid. Often, it is a gray square as shown here.

   iii. Note that some sections may be filled in.

> ▸ When sections are filled in, it means one of two things:

>> – the robot cannot go to those parts of the grid (often filled in with black, comparable to walls in a maze).

>> – the robot is trying to go to that part of the grid (filled in with gray).

>> – the question would explain what each color represents.

3. The best way to prepare for these types of questions is to do the following:

   i. Practice writing code that creates visual movement.

   ii. Plan out what motion looks like without using a computer. Write driving directions or steps to move from one spot to another in your neighborhood and then ask a friend or family member to try them out. Try to use the robot operations from the chart below.

> ▸ Ask the person who tried them to evaluate them: Did they work? Were they detailed enough?

> ▸ Consider how you might improve them. Could you use a loop or selection statements?

4. Here are some more details about robot operations.

How this would be used on the exam:	Instruction in Text	Instruction in Block
The robot moves one square forward in the direction it is facing.	MOVE_FORWARD()	MOVE_FORWARD
The robot rotates 90 degrees counterclockwise (turns left of direction facing).	ROTATE_LEFT()	ROTATE_LEFT
The robot rotates 90 degrees clockwise (turns right of direction facing).	ROTATE_RIGHT()	ROTATE_RIGHT
Evaluates to true if there is an open square one square in the direction. Otherwise, evaluates to false. The value of direction can be left, right, backward, or forward.	CAN_MOVE(direction)	CAN_MOVE(direction)

EXAMPLE 18:

The following question uses a robot in a grid of squares. The robot is represented as a triangle, which is initially in the top left square facing up.

If you want the robot to end up in the bottom right square facing up, write steps/pseudocode to make this happen. Try to use ROBOT procedures as much as possible.

Answer:

There are many! Some might be more complicated than others.

In your first approach, you might have said:	Notice how this could be reduced to the following:

```
ROTATE RIGHT

MOVE FORWARD

MOVE FORWARD

MOVE FORWARD

MOVE FORWARD

ROTATE RIGHT

MOVE FORWARD

MOVE FORWARD

MOVE FORWARD

MOVE FORWARD

ROTATE RIGHT

ROTATE RIGHT
```

```
ROTATE_RIGHT()

REPEAT 4 TIMES

    MOVE_FORWARD()

ROTATE_RIGHT()

REPEAT 4 TIMES

    MOVE_FORWARD()

REPEAT 2 TIMES

    ROTATE RIGHT
```

EXAMPLE 19 (SNEAK PEEK):

Two different starting positions of a robot are shown below. For both positions, robots are initially facing up. The robot can move into a white or gray square, but cannot move into a black region.

POSITION I:

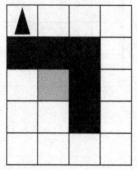

POSITION II:

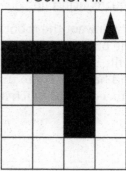

The program below was written to move the robot to the gray square. The program uses the procedure Goal_Reached(), which evaluates to true if the robot is in the gray square and evaluates to false otherwise.

```
REPEAT UNTIL Goal_Reached () {
  IF CAN_MOVE(forward) {
    REPEAT UNTIL (NOT(CAN_MOVE(forward))
      MOVE_FORWARD()
  }
  ELSE
  {
    IF CAN_MOVE(right) {
      ROTATE_RIGHT()
      REPEAT UNTIL (NOT(CAN_MOVE(forward))
        MOVE_FORWARD()
    }
    ELSE {
      ROTATE_LEFT()
      REPEAT UNTIL (NOT(CAN_MOVE(forward))
        MOVE_FORWARD()
    }
  }
}
```

Using the code above, which starting position would cause the robot to move correctly to the gray square?

(A) Either Position I or Position II

(B) Neither Position I or Position II

(C) Position I only

(D) Position II only

Answer: (A)

Either Position I or Position II would work. The best way to see each of these is to place your pencil (or a small object) onto the grid and move it as the code specifies. Starting from Position II results in the robot moving left, turning around, then following the path in Position I.

IV. SUMMARY

A. The Exam Reference Sheet is a summary of the type of programming instructions that will be used on the End-of-Course Exam.

   1. The instructions will be block-based or text-based.

   2. The instructions are organized into eight categories.

B. The best way to learn programming is to practice programming by solving problems on a computer.

C. It is important to practice the coding style and different types of exam questions.

   1. See Chapter 19 for more multiple-choice questions.

   2. Take our online practice exam available at *www.rea.com/ studycenter*.

Big Idea 1: Creative Development

Chapter

I. OVERVIEW

A. About 10%–13% of the End-of-Course Exam questions will focus on Creative Development.

B. This means you can expect 7–9 questions on your exam to focus on this topic.

C. In addition, when you are collaborating with others or planning programming projects, you should be practicing many of the ideas from this topic.

D. Here are some questions you can ask yourself throughout the year to prepare to answer questions you will see in the End-of-Course Exam:

1. How has working with other people improved your projects?

2. What did you learn from working with others that you could not have learned on your own?

3. What are some ways you can get additional feedback or ideas, while you are coding, to improve your projects?

4. What is a good approach to planning (before you code) that has worked for you?

5. What apps or programs have you stopped using because you did not like the design or how you needed to interact with it?

II. **WHAT IS CREATIVE DEVELOPMENT?**

A. Creative Development describes the processes used by people to create computing innovations.

B. Creative Development involves all of the following:

1. Planning—deciding what you want to code before you begin programming

2. Collaboration—working with others to include multiple perspectives and approaches in your solution

3. Testing—being sure the code works as intended

4. Debugging—fixing mistakes or issues that surface while testing

5. Reflecting—thinking about what worked and what did not

III. **WHAT YOU NEED TO KNOW ABOUT CREATIVE DEVELOPMENT**

A. Computing innovations are innovations that include a program as an integral part of its function.

B. Computing innovations can be physical, nonphysical computing software, or a nonphysical computing concept. Here are some examples provided by the College Board:

1. physical computing innovations: smartphone, wireless router, 3D printer, self-driving car

2. nonphysical computing innovations: facial-recognition software, picture-editing software

3. nonphysical computing concept: social media, e-commerce

4. non-computing innovations: computer mouse, microwave oven, sensor

C. When programming, practice using the following key words:

1. program: collection of program statements that perform a task

2. code segment: collection of program statements that are part of a larger program

3. input: data sent to the program to be processed

4. event: an action that supplies input data to a program (examples: mouse click, button press)

5. event-driven programming: when program statements are triggered by events rather than sequential flow of control

6. output: data sent from program to a device (often influenced by input)

7. program requirements: how the program should behave

   i. Often includes expected inputs and outputs

   ii. May be called program specifications

8. program documentation: description of how a code segment worked and how it was developed

   i. Comments: type of documentation written into program to be read by other programmers; do not impact how code runs

   ii. Documentation should happen throughout development whether you are working independently or collaboratively

 IV. WHAT YOU NEED TO UNDERSTAND ABOUT CREATIVE DEVELOPMENT

A. Collaboration is an essential part of building computing innovations.

B. Collaboration helps with all of the following design and programming issues:

1. Bias

   i. more perspectives mean fewer people will be left out of planning and testing

   ii. when more perspectives are included, usually this leads to fewer biases being included in the program

2. User experiences

   i. including information gathered from users helps include more perspectives

   ii. this should help in designing applications to include more people

C. Development can be ordered (with a series of steps you plan to take) or more exploratory (where you create and see what happens as a result).

D. Typical phases of development:

1. Investigating and reflecting—researching, learning about the problem, understanding the desired solution and the constraints; examples include:

   i.   collecting data through surveys

   ii. user testing

   iii. interviews

   iv. direct observation

2. Designing—planning the desired solution, communicating with people about the design; steps include:

   i.   brainstorming

   ii. planning and storyboarding

   iii. organizing the program into smaller parts

    iv. creating diagrams to represent logic and/or appearance of interface

    v. plan for how program will be tested

    vi. pseudocode can help in this stage

       ▸ Pseudocode is shorthand for code.

       ▸ Often, pseudocode shows the steps and order of an algorithm.

3. Prototyping—trying out different parts of the solution to see if these parts will work.

    i. In this step, you are writing code.

    ii. To write code you need:

       ▸ A programming language

       ▸ A development environment

4. Testing—inputs should check that the algorithm or program is producing expected outcomes.

    i. Results from testing are used to revise algorithms and programs.

    ii. When choosing inputs, they should be at or just beyond the extremes (minimum and maximum) of possible input data.

    iii. Testing should be planned to be sure program requirements are met by the program.

    iv. There are four types of errors:

       ▸ Syntax errors

          – Syntax is "grammar" in an algorithm.

          – A syntax error means you tried to do something that your programming language does not understand.

          – Code will usually not run with a syntax error; it is often caught by your development environment.

▸ Logical error

– Your code does not do what you intended it to do.

– To catch these errors, you need to test your code.

– The best way to test code is to be sure you choose inputs that will reach all of the possible logical paths the code could take.

▸ Run-time error

– Mistake in program happens when you are running code.

– Often causes program to stop running.

– Each language defines their own run-time errors.

▸ Overflow error

– Mistake that happens when computer attempts to handle a number that is outside its defined set of values.

– If a computer tries to store a number that is larger than its maximum value, this would be an overflow error.

E. There are two main styles of software development: iterative and incremental.

1. Iterative development

   i. Requires regular feedback, testing, and reflection throughout the development process.

   ii. Often requires revisiting earlier phases of process.

2. Incremental development

   i. Breaking problem into smaller pieces.

   ii. Making sure each piece works before adding it to the whole.

For examples of different development models, look up *Waterfall Software Development* and *Agile Software Development*. Waterfall tends to be more incremental and Agile tends to be more iterative.

EXAMPLE 1 (SNEAK PEEK):

A person collaborates with others to develop a program. One day per week, customers test the working parts of the program and provide feedback to developers. On a daily basis, developers meet to discuss challenges and possible solutions as well as progress made. Then, developers work to meet the needs of the user, customer, and their development team. This will continue throughout the development of a software project.

What is the best term for the development process that is being used?

(A) Incremental development

(B) Iterative development

(C) Designing

(D) Testing

Answer: (B)

The answer is Choice (B). Notice that the developer is meeting with many people on a regular basis to get feedback and to reflect on that feedback. This is typical iterative development. Choice (A) is not correct because incremental development would involve less feedback, especially from the user. Choice (C) is not correct because the developer is coding actively. While redesign may be needed if something goes wrong, the developer is prototyping (testing small versions with the customer), not designing. Choice (D) is not correct because the developer is still meeting regularly with the team and showing small pieces to the customer. The developer is not strictly testing.

V. WHAT YOU NEED TO BE ABLE TO DO WITH CREATIVE DEVELOPMENT

A. It is important that you practice collaboration so you can explain how it works.

   1. Two ways to practice collaboration are through:

      i. Pair programming

      ii. Using online tools such as GitHub and/or video conferencing

   2. While collaborating, you will need to practice interpersonal skills such as:

      i. Communication—being sure your voice is being heard and you are listening to the opinions of others

      ii. Consensus building—using shared voices to reach agreements

      iii. Conflict resolution—if there is a difference of opinion, you work together to weigh options and decide the best course of action

      iv. Negotiation:

         ▸ Your relationship with your partner is important, but reaching agreement is critical as well.

         ▸ To successfully negotiate you try to find a way where both members of your team can be equally satisfied (and sometimes dissatisfied) so progress can still be made on the project.

VI. PAIR PROGRAMMING

A. What is Pair Programming?

   1. Pair Programming is an approach to collaboration where:

      i. One person is the "driver," so in charge of the hardware (the mouse, the keyboard, etc.). The driver's main jobs are to:

> ‣ talk the navigator through each step of the plan.

> ‣ make sure the navigator understands and is engaged with the plan.

> ‣ follow the plan, including testing.

ii. One person is the "navigator," so in charge of the plan. The navigator's main jobs are to:

> ‣ communicate if you are in agreement with what is happening.

> ‣ be sure you are engaged with the code.

> ‣ be sure you are both following the plan, including testing.

iii. Both people share:

> ‣ the monitor.

> ‣ the responsibility of creating the plan.

> ‣ a plan for how often roles will change.

iv. Pair programming works really well if you are:

> ‣ learning programming for the first time.

> ‣ learning a new language for the first time.

> ‣ trying to do something you have not done before that has a lot of steps.

B. Industry professionals use it when adding new features or when changes are particularly complex.

C. Here are some "best practices" you should use to have a good experience with pair programming:

1. Plan ahead:

   i. Decide on the shared plan.

   ii. Decide who will navigate and who will drive.

   iii. Decide how often you will change roles.

2. If you notice a member of the team (driver or navigator) needs some encouragement, here are some questions you could ask:

    i. What should we do next?

    ii. How would you solve this?

3. Communicate your needs to the best of your ability. Some possible needs are:

    i. You need a little more time to think.

    ii. You would like to talk more together before coding changes are being made.

    iii. You notice your partner made a decision; you want to understand why/how they made that choice so you can learn from it.

    iv. You notice it is time to change roles.

Test Tip

If this is your first time using pair programming, be patient. While it may seem to take a little longer, both partners will grow from this. All programmers improve their skills working with others and will be in a better position to explain coding decisions they have made.

D. When you are writing programs, you should be able to explain how a program or code segment (part of the program) functions.

E. When you are testing programs, you should have multiple strategies to find and correct errors. Some of these are:

1. using test cases (inputs that test different segments of code)

2. hand tracing (diagramming the logic/path code travels to process inputs)

3. visualizations (flowcharting, diagrams)

4. debuggers (tools that come with development environments that let you see how variables are being defined and memory is allocated while code is running)

5. adding extra output statements (displaying more so you can see how variables are being defined and changed)

EXAMPLE 2 (SNEAK PEEK):

The following code segment is intended to set max equal to the maximum value among the integer variables a, b, and c. The code segment does not work as intended in all cases.

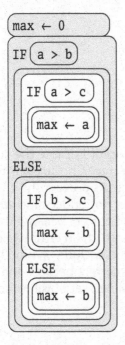

Which of the following initial values for a, b, and c can be used to show that the code segment does not work as intended?

(A) a = 5, b = 4, c = 4

(B) a = 4, b = 3, c = 5

(C) a = 4, b = 5, c = 5

(D) a = 3, b = 4, c = 5

Answer: (B)

Trace Choice (B). Since 4 is greater than 3, the outer IF condition is true. However, the inner condition is false, so max will not be assigned. Since the outer IF was true, the code following the ELSE would not run and max would remain at its original value of 0. Trace Choices (A), (C), and (D) and notice that they appear to work as they all assign the correct value to max.

EXAMPLE 3 (SNEAK PEEK):

Consider the error in Example 2. What type of error was this?

(A) Logic error

(B) Syntax error

(C) Run-time error

(D) Overflow error

Answer: (A)

Choice (A) is correct. This is a logic error because the code will run, but it does not behave as expected. Choice (B) is not correct because the code did run. Syntax errors prevent the code from running because the computer does not understand what you are asking it to do. Choice (C) is not correct because there is no error that would cause the code to return an error while running. Common examples of run-time errors include division by 0 or out-of-bounds errors. Choice (D) is not correct because the numbers 3, 4, and 5 are certainly within the defined set of values so this is not an overflow error.

Test Tip

Remember, the best way to practice Creative Development is to program. Choose interesting ideas to implement in your coding language of choice and make them happen. While creating these ideas, practice using the words, concepts, and skills from this chapter and you will be well prepared for questions in your End-of-Course Exam related to this topic.

Big Idea 2: Data

I. OVERVIEW

A. About 17%–22% of the End-of-Course Exam questions will focus on Data.

B. This means you can expect 12–15 questions on your exam to focus on this topic.

C. Here are some questions you can ask yourself to prepare to answer questions you will see in the End-of-Course Exam:

1. How can we use 1s and 0s to represent something complex like an image or a video?

2. How can you use data from social media to predict the number of people who will attend a school event?

3. When is it more appropriate to use a computer and when is it more appropriate to do work on paper?

4. How can you adjust data to make it easier for a computer to analyze it?

II. WHAT IS DATA?

A. Data is the information that is inputted, outputted, and/or transformed by any computer program.

B. Data scientists use computing and existing data to create new understandings. This is an essential field in our world because of the following:

1. We have more data than ever available to us for entertainment, decision making, and problem solving.

2. As this data increases so does our need to understand patterns and display conclusions.

III. WHAT YOU NEED TO KNOW ABOUT DATA

A. Vocabulary related to binary numbers:

- binary number system—number system consisting of two digits: 0 or 1

- bit—short for binary digit; either a 0 or a 1

- byte—8 bits

- decimal number system—number system consisting of ten digits: 0, 1, 2, 3, 4, 5, 6, 7, 8, and 9

B. Vocabulary related to data compression:

- analog data—continuous data

  - examples: volume of music, position of a sprinter during a race, colors in a painting

- data compression—approach to storing or transmitting data that is intended to reduce the number of bits required for the data

  - lossless data compression algorithms— usually reduces the number of bits stored or transmitted; guarantees complete reconstruction of original data

  - lossy data compression algorithms— significantly reduces the number of bits stored or transmitted; only allow reconstruction of an approximation of the original data

▸ digital data—data that has values that are sampled discretely

   – examples: mp3 sound files, YouTube videos

▸ sampling technique—used to translate analog data to digital data;

   – usually means samples of analog data are taken at regular intervals

C. Vocabulary related to extracting information from data:

▸ information—collection of patterns and/or facts extracted from data

▸ correlation—there seems to be a pattern between two variables in a data set

   – positive correlation—one variable increases when a second variable increases

   – negative correlation—one variable increases when a second variable decreases

▸ causation—one variable impacts a second variable's behavior; the second variable *depends* on the first

▸ metadata—data about data

   – example: a piece of data may be a video you found on YouTube, but the metadata may be the date the video was published or the file size

▸ cleaning data—changing a data set so the data can be processed without changing its meaning

   – example: replacing "none" with 0 or changing all state abbreviations to capital letters

▸ bias—caused when the data sample is not random

IV. **WHAT YOU NEED TO UNDERSTAND AND BE ABLE TO DO WITH DATA**

A. Explain how data can be represented using bits.

B. All data stored in a computer eventually becomes a binary digit.

C. Understanding the Decimal (Base-10) Number System

1. Consider the number 167 in our number system. You would say it as "one hundred sixty-seven." When you say it, you hear the *worth* of the 1 is much greater (1 *hundred*) than that of the 6 or the 7. The place value increases from right to left and place value matters much more than the digits themselves.

2. In our base-10 system we have 10 digits: 0, 1, 2, 3, 4, 5, 6, 7, 8, and 9. In any number system that we will discuss for this course, place value increases from right to left. Notice that each place value is a power of 10 higher than the place value to its right.

100	10	1
1	6	7

3. Writing this out: $167 = 1*10^2 + 6*10^1 + 7*10^0$

4. You might see the number 167 in terms of its place value or the "bucket" each digit is placed in to tell you its worth.

5. Let's think about the word "digit." As humans, we have 10 digits (fingers) and we have been taught from a young age to count to 10 on these fingers. The problem with this is that the last number (10) involves *two* digits (0 and 1). Instead, our ten digits are 0, 1, 2, 3, 4, 5, 6, 7, 8, 9. In fact, all number systems will start with the number 0.

D. Counting in our (Base-10) Number System

1. Notice how when we run out of digits (we reach 9), a new digit is added to the left of the 9 and the place value that held the 9 is reset to 0.

2. This would happen again at 19. 19 + 1 = 20. The place value that held the 9 becomes a 0 and the place value to the left of the 9 is increased by 1.

3. The hundreds place needs to be introduced for the first time to handle 99 + 1. Since both the ones and the tens place are "filled" with the largest digit, the hundreds place is needed: 99 + 1 = 100.

4. Writing this out:

   0, 1, 2, 3, 4, 5, 6, 7, 8, 9, 10, . . ., 19, 20, . . . 29, 30, . . . 99, 100, . . . 999, 1000

5. As numbers increase in value, change to each number happens by increasing place value from right to left.

   i.   After 98 is 99. The rightmost place value increases by 1.

   ii. After 99 is 100.

   ▸ If the place value on the right runs out of digits, the place value just to its left takes over.

   ▸ If needed, a new place value is introduced.

   iii. Notice: 9 + 1 = 10.

E. Counting in the Binary Number (Base-2) System

1. Counting in the base-2 system is very different from our number system. To start, there are two digits: 0 and 1.

2. Remember how our number system handled 9 (introduction of a new place value *and* resetting the 9's place value to 0)? Let's think about what that looks like in binary:

   i.   0—the first number (and digit) in any number system

   ii. 1—the second number in any number system

   iii. 10—we ran out of digits so we need a new place value

   iv. 11—increment place value on the right first

   v.   100—ran out of digits so we need a new place value

3. Notice that in binary: 1 + 1 = 10.

4. Binary numbers require a lot more place values to express a value than we need in the decimal number system.

F. Converting Decimal (Base-10) to Binary (Base-2)

1. To understand how to convert this value to a different number system, we have to think of numbers in terms of the "buckets" or place values. The place values we are used to understanding are powers of 10. Remember 167. See image at right. $10^0 = 1$, $10^1 = 10$, and $10^2 = 100$.

100	10	1
1	6	7

2. Suppose we want to convert 167 to binary digits (or "bits").

   i. We will need to think in powers of 2. $2^0 = 1$, $2^1 = 2$, $2^2 = 4$, $2^3 = 8$, and so on. 256 is a power of 2 that is too large for 167, so this will be an unnecessary place value.

   ii. The next lowest is 128. $167 - 128 = 39$.

   iii. So we will need to find digits to hold a value of 39.

   iv. Continuing to fill place values from left to right, the next place value is worth 64. Since 39 is less than 64, we cannot use that place value.

   v. Looking to 32, we will use that place value. This pattern continues until the total value of 167 is stored in binary digits.

256	128	64	32	16	8	4	2	1
0	1	0	1	0	0	1	1	1

   vi. So decimal value 167 is equivalent to 10100111 in binary.

vii. Try this out on a separate piece of paper by following these steps:

STEP 1: Write a table of place values (powers of two).

- Place values increase from right to left.

- The highest power of 2 is the highest number that can go into the value you are trying to convert without going over it.

STEP 2: Fill in 1 or 0 from left to right.

- If the place value is used (number is a 1) then subtract from the original value.

- Repeat until each position has a 1 or 0.

STEP 3: The number on the bottom of the table is a binary representation of the original value.

G. Converting Binary to Decimal

1. Based on the above, we know that 167 in decimal digits is equivalent to 10100111. We can convert back from binary digits to the decimal number system:

$$10100111 = 1(2^7) + 0(2^6) + 1(2^5) + 0(2^4) + 0(2^3) + 1(2^2) + 1(2^1) + 1(2^0)$$
$$= 128 + 0 + 32 + 0 + 0 + 4 + 2 + 1 = 167$$

Test Tip

In the End-of-Course Exam, all of the binary numbers you will see will be 8 bits (1 byte) or less. Therefore, the largest binary value you will see would be 11111111. This is equivalent to 128 + 64 + 32 + 16 + 8 + 4 + 2 + 1 = 255 in base 10.

EXAMPLE 1 (SNEAK PEEK):

A computer program encodes book ID numbers in binary. The first book was assigned 1110011. The second book was assigned 1110100. The third book was assigned 1110101. Following this pattern, what ID will be assigned to the fourth book?

  (A) 1110110

  (B) 1111101

  (C) 1110111

  (D) 1110101

Answer: (A)

Notice that each book is going up by 1. Remember that in binary, 1 + 1 = 10. So, add 1 to the ID for the third book to get the ID for the fourth book. See addition work shown to the right.

$$\begin{array}{r} 11 \\ 1110011 \\ +\qquad 1 \\ \hline 1110100 \end{array}$$

H. Number Systems are different in computers.

  1. Computers do not have an infinite number of place values.

  2. This means you will hit a limit as numbers increase or decrease.

  i.   This limit is different for every programming language.

  ii. Going beyond the limit leads to errors in the language.

  iii. This is called an overflow error.

  3. You will need to show you understand that these limits exist.

EXAMPLE 2 (SNEAK PEEK):

Refer to Example 1. The computer system limits the book ID so it will be no more than 7 bits in length. How many book IDs can the system support?

(A) 1024

(B) 512

(C) 256

(D) 128

Answer: (D)

With 1 bit, two IDs are possible: 0 or 1. With 2 bits, four IDs are possible: 00, 01, 10, or 11. With 3 bits, eight bits are possible: 000, 001, 010, 100, 011, 110, 101, or 111. Notice the pattern. With n bits, 2^n IDs would be possible. The correct answer is (D). For 7 bits, $2^7 = 128$ IDs are possible.

EXAMPLE 3 (SNEAK PEEK):

Refer to Examples 1 and 2. What is the largest book ID possible using this 7-bit system?

(A) 511

(B) 255

(C) 127

(D) 128

Answer: (C)

Notice the pattern discussed above. With 2 bits, four IDs are possible: 00, 01, 10, or 11. The largest ID would be binary number 11. Converting 11 to decimal, $1(2^1) + 1(2^0) = 2 + 1 = 3$. With 3 bits, the largest ID was binary number 111. Converting 111 to decimal, $1(2^2) + 1(2^1) + 1(2^0) = 4 + 2 + 1 = 7$. Notice the pattern. With n bits, the largest ID would be $2^n - 1$. The correct answer is (C). For 7 bits, the largest ID is $2^7 - 1 = 127$.

I. Groups of binary digits represent more complicated data values like characters, color, and numbers.

    1. This is an example of abstraction (reducing complexity).

    2. Color, letter, or number are higher levels of abstractions.

    3. The lowest level of abstraction are the binary digits that represent that color, letter, or number.

EXAMPLE 4:

4a. ASCII is the encoding scheme used to represent characters as a number. An example of this scheme is the uppercase letter "B" represented by "66" in base-10. How would the letter be represented in its lowest level of abstraction?

4b. RGB (Red, Green, Blue) values are used to encode color as a number. An early RGB encoding scheme used 8 bits (3 for red, 3 for green, 2 for blue). How many different colors (called a palette) could be created with this scheme?

4c. The current RGB scheme uses 24 bits per color. It is called "True Color" because there are so many colors in this palette that images created using it look more real.

Which of the following best describes the result of using 24-bit RGB encoding instead of 8 bit RGB encoding?

    (A) 3 times as many values can be represented

    (B) 2^{16} times as many values can be represented

    (C) 16^3 as many values can be represented

    (D) 16 times as many values can be represented

Answers:

4a. The lowest level abstraction of a number is binary. 66 is 64 + 2, so in binary 66 is 1000010.

4b. 8 bits means that in each bit there are 2 possibilities (1 or 0). So there are 2^8 possible combinations. $2^8 = 256$. There are 256 colors possible in the RGB palette. Eventually, at its lower level, colors would be represented in binary digits, or bits from 00000000 to 11111111.

4c. 24 bit RGB encoding means 2^{24} colors can be represented. The color palette has 2^{24} distinct colors. This is $\dfrac{2^{24}}{2^8} = 2^{(24-8)} = 2^{16}$ times as many colors as the 8 bit RGB palette. Choice (B) is correct.

J. Explain that the way data is processed in a program might be different from the way it looks on the outside to a program user.

1. Data compression algorithms are often applied to data in a program.

2. You can use data compression algorithms to reduce the size of data files you are sharing with others.

3. There are two types of data compression algorithms: Lossless vs. Lossy

   i. Lossless compression algorithms

   ▸ usually reduce the number of bits stored

   ▸ guarantee you can recreate the data after it has been compressed

   ▸ examples of lossless file extensions: .zip, .png, .gif

   ▸ used if being able to reconstruct the data matters more than the compression amount

   ii. Lossy compression algorithms

   ▸ can significantly reduce the number of bits stored

   ▸ only allow reconstruction of approximation of the original data

   ▸ examples of lossy file extensions: .jpg, .mp3, .mpeg

   ▸ used if the compression amount matters more than being able to recreate the data

EXAMPLE 5 (SNEAK PEEK):

A teacher asked a student to email data files with different parts of a project about a scientific experiment. Which data file would most likely be shared using lossy compression?

    (A) The document with the written report

    (B) The spreadsheet that contains the data analysis

    (C) The slide deck that explains the results

    (D) The image showing the experiment setup

Answer: (D)

Choice (D) is correct because, of all the files, that is most likely the largest in size. Without the student choosing lossy compression, images are often stored as jpg files. To make viewing the project easiest for the teacher, the document, spreadsheet, and slide deck would likely be stored in their original format.

K. Programs can be used to process data, allowing users to discover information and create new knowledge.

    1. Correlation does not imply causation.

        i. It is possible that one variable seems related to another variable.

        ii. For example, suppose one morning you kept track of the number of cars parked on your street.

You created the following graph:

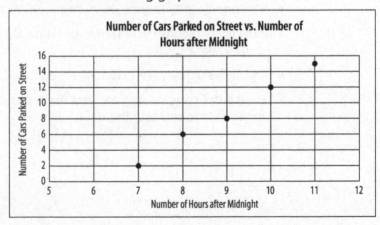

- You notice that there is a correlation (relationship) between the number of hours after midnight and the number of cars parked on the street.

- The correlation is positive because as the number of hours increases, the number of cars also increases.

- The correlation is linear because the slope seems constant.

- However, this does not mean causation.

  - The number of cars parked on the street may or may not depend on the number of hours after midnight.

  - To prove causation you need a carefully designed experiment where everything that could be randomized is randomized.

- Sometimes a computer is used to simulate that experiment. In that case, the experiment is called a simulation.

2. Data often needs to come from multiple sources to draw conclusions.

3. Metadata can be helpful.

   i. For example, if you have a spreadsheet of data, examples of metadata include: date of last file modification, name of file creator, file extension, or file size.

   ii. Metadata can help you to organize, find, and manage information.

4. Processing data comes with separate challenges.

   i. The data set needs to be cleaned before you can use it. Examples look like:

      - A few people entered text when they should have entered numbers.

      - Some people used abbreviations while others typed a full name.

ii. The data set is incomplete; some people did not answer questions.

iii. The data set is invalid.

iv. The data set needs to be combined with another data set to complete the analysis.

v. There is a bias in the type or source of the data.

- ▸ This cannot be fixed by collecting more data.

- ▸ To fix this, you often need to redesign the study and use new data sources.

vi. The data set is too large to be processed with a single computer.

- ▸ May require parallel systems

- ▸ This is why it is important to consider scalability with data sets and data studies. When designing a data study, be sure the system can handle the size and calculation requirements of the study.

EXAMPLE 6 (SNEAK PEEK):

A scientist is interested in using a flower application to study flowers that are in bloom over a large geographic area. The application is capable of:

- – Storing the image of the flower.

- – Running a procedure that uses image recognition to identify the flower's scientific name.

- – Creating a database that contains the flower's scientific name, a timestamp of when the image was taken, and the flower's location where the image was taken.

6a. Which of the following questions about flowers could NOT be answered using *only* the data collected within this database?

(A) What is the most frequent flower type in a geographic area?

(B) When are flowers most likely to be in bloom in a geographic area?

(C) What was the temperature on the day the image was taken?

(D) What time of day are images of flowers most likely to be taken?

6b. The scientist wants to encourage many people to use this app to collect patterns of flower growth over many years. How might the scientist describe the data collection process to others?

I. This is an example of crowdsourcing. Many people are improving the application.

II. This is an example of citizen science. Many people are collecting data for this scientific study.

III. This is an example of using metadata. The database has a timestamp for each data point collected.

(A) I and II

(B) I, II, and III

(C) II only

(D) I and III

6c. What is a likely decision that was made about the data stored on this database? Select *two* answers.

(A) It is likely that this database uses lossy compression for the GPS coordinates of each flower.

(B) It is likely that the server that contains this database is the scientist's personal computer.

(C) It is likely that the flower images are stored using lossy compression.

(D) It is likely that each item of the database will be stored using a new variable name.

Answers:

6a. (C) The data stored does not include temperature.

6b. (C) This is citizen science; many people are contributing to a scientific study. This is not crowdsourcing. There is no evidence that these results will be used to modify the application or that people will be able to contribute to modifying the application. It may be that the application will not change at all from the start to the end of this study. The timestamp is not necessarily metadata. It could be that the application pulls the timestamp from the image. However, the application itself could be responsible for generating the timestamp. An example of metadata for the database might be the name of the database or the date that the database was created.

6c. (C), (D) Choice (A) is incorrect because GPS coordinates need to be stored with accuracy to be valuable. Lossy compression means that there is a chance that the data could only be partially restored. This would not be a risk worth taking for the GPS coordinates. Choice (B) is incorrect because it is not likely that the database would be housed on a personal computer because of space and security concerns. Choice (C) is correct because the flower images would be larger than other data points and likely already captured using lossy compression such as a jpeg file type. Choice (D) is correct. The collection of image files might be stored under a variable called "images", for example.

Test Tip

Notice how one specific example leads to several related multiple-choice questions. You will see this throughout the End-of-Course Exam. It is best to not jump around if you have a chain of questions related to one situation. Once you understand the context, answer all the questions related to it.

EXAMPLE 7 (SNEAK PEEK):

A computer simulation of operations at a grocery store with several automated check-out stations is run several times. In each run of the simulation, only the number of stations is changed. Which of the following changes is most likely to occur between runs of the simulation? Select *two* answers.

(A) A change in the average length of time needed to complete the transaction once a person enters the line to wait

(B) A change in the amount of bags needed for the groceries per transaction

(C) A change in the amount of transactions completed in the store per hour

(D) A change in the price of the groceries per transaction

Answer: (A), (C)

Choices (A) and (C) are related to the number of stations. As stations increase or decrease, both the average wait time and the number of transactions would be impacted. Choices (B) and (D) are not correct because neither of these things are related to the number of stations. So, they would not be a change made between runs in this simulation.

Test Tip

To prepare for multiple-choice questions related to data, read about data studies that have led to changes in our world and consider doing your own studies. Consider a possible relationship between two variables that you want to investigate further in your personal life or in your school. Collect data, clean the data if needed, use other data sources, and perform an analysis. Think about what you learned from this as well as what you would do differently.

Big Idea 3: Algorithms & Programming

16

I. OVERVIEW

A. About 30%–35% of the End-of-Course Exam questions will focus on Algorithms & Programming.

B. This means you can expect 21–25 questions on your exam to focus on this topic.

C. Here are some questions you can ask yourself throughout the year to prepare to answer questions you will see in the End-of-Course Exam:

1. How is data stored in a program?

2. What might happen if you completed steps in your regular afternoon routine in a different order? How might this change impact your preparation for the following day?

3. How do games connect player actions to button presses? How do applications decide what should be a button press and what should be data you need to input?

4. What types of problems are easier to solve with a computer and what types of problems cannot be solved with a computer? Why?

II. WHAT ARE ALGORITHMS AND PROGRAMMING?

A. Algorithms are the step-by-step instructions written in a programming language.

B. Programming is the act of creating code that instructs a computer to do tasks including:

1. simulate something to help us understand our world.

2. automate a repeated action to make us more efficient problem solvers.

3. create a new game that will entertain us.

C. Programming allows us to test, run, analyze, and improve on algorithms.

D. All languages, whether block-based or text-based, have similar programming structures and commands.

III. WHAT YOU NEED TO KNOW ABOUT ALGORITHMS AND PROGRAMMING

A. Related to Variables and Assignments

▸ variable: a named memory location inside a program; could hold a single value or a list of values

   − Boolean variable: a variable that is either true or false

▸ list: ordered sequence of elements

   − element: an individual value in a list

   − index: the location of a value in a list

   − traversing a list: accessing all elements in a list

▸ string: ordered sequence of characters

   − string concatenation: joins together two or more strings end-to-end to make a new string

   − substring: part of existing string

B. Related to Expressions

▸ data abstraction:

- examples of data abstraction: name for a list, name for a value stored in program

- these are abstractions because you can reference a variable name without knowing the values stored there

▸ algorithm: set of instructions to accomplish a specific task

▸ code statement: part of the program that expresses an action

▸ expression: can be a value, variable, operator, or a procedure call that returns a value

▸ relational operator: used to test relationship between two variables

- returns true if the relationship is true; false otherwise

- the following relational operators exist in the End-of-Course Exam: =, ≠, <, ≤, >, and ≥

▸ logical operator: used to test logical relationship between two Boolean expressions

- returns true if relationship is true; false otherwise

- the following logical operators exist in the End-of-Course Exam: AND, OR, NOT

▸ sequencing: application of each step of an algorithm in the order in which the code statements are given

C. Related to Conditionals

▸ conditional statements ("if-statements"): causes program to execute only certain statements

- to run code in a conditional statement, the Boolean expression must be satisfied

- conditionals can be "nested," meaning a conditional can be inside of a conditional statement

> ▸ conditional statements control "selection" in an algorithm

>> – code that is executed is determined by whether or not an expression evaluates to `true` or `false`

>> – selection is one of three key parts (sequence, selection, and iteration) of any algorithm; selection is controlled by conditional statements

D. Related to Iteration

> ▸ iteration: a repeating part of an algorithm

> ▸ iteration changes the sequential flow of control by repeating a set of statements zero or more times or until a condition is met

E. Related to Search Algorithms

> ▸ linear (or sequential) search: checks each element of a list, in order, until the desired value is found or all the elements in the list have been checked

> ▸ binary search:

>> – requires a sorted data set

>> – starts in the middle of the set, eliminates half of the data, and repeats until the desired value is found or all elements have been eliminated

> ▸ binary search is often more efficient than linear search for large data sets

F. Related to Procedures

> ▸ procedure: named group of programming instructions

>> – may have parameters and a return value

>> – may be called method or function, depending on the language

> ▸ parameters: input variables of a procedure

> ▸ arguments: the values of the parameters when the procedure is called

- modularity: the breaking down of a program into separate subprograms

- software library: group of procedures that may be used to create programs

  - Application Program Interfaces (APIs) are documents that contain the "rules" for how you can use procedures in a library

    a. help you know how procedures in a library behave and can be used

    b. often available online; for most languages, you can find them using an online search tool. For example, to find Python's API, you can type "Python API" or "Python Reference Documents" into your favorite search engine.

  - If new libraries are created, documentation should clarify behaviors of procedures and how to use them.

G. Related to Algorithms

- simulation: abstractions of more complicated objects or problems created for a specific purpose

- random number generators: simulate randomness in a program

- problem: a task that may or may not be solvable using an algorithm

- decision problem: problem with a yes or no answer

- optimization problem: problem with the goal of finding the "best" solution among many (example: What is the least number of steps a robot would need to take to move from point A to point B?)

- instance (of a problem): a problem with specific input

  - example of a problem: finding the maximum of a list of integers

  - instance of this problem: finding the maximum of the list {3, 6, 4, 2}

▸ efficiency: estimation of the amount of resources needed by an algorithm

   – often expressed as a function of the size of the input

   – determined through formal (mathematical) reasoning

   – can be informally measured by determining the number of times a statement or group of statements executes

▸ reasonable time: algorithms with efficiency that is polynomial or slower

   – ex: constant, linear, square, cube, etc.

▸ unreasonable time: algorithms with exponential or factorial efficiencies

   – ex: many optimization problems like the traveling salesperson

▸ heuristic: an approach that produces a solution to problems that do not generally have a solution in reasonable time

   – solution is not guaranteed to be optimal (the best)

   – may be used to find a solution even if it is not the best

▸ decidable problem: decision problem for which an algorithm can be written to answer "yes" or "no" for all inputs

▸ undecidable problem: problem for which no algorithm can be constructed that is capable of answering "yes" or "no" for all inputs

   – may have some instances where a decision can be made

   – no single solution will solve all instances

 IV. WHAT YOU NEED TO UNDERSTAND ABOUT ALGORITHMS AND PROGRAMMING

A. Programmers represent and organize data in many ways.

   1. This allows programmers to find specific solutions to generalizable problems.

2. Some tips:

   i. Use variable names that help make your code readable.

      ▸ If you are writing code about a number, use number or num as the variable name rather than a generic letter like x.

      ▸ If you are writing code that contains a list, use a word that tells you what is stored in the list. For example, a good name for a list of dates would be dates.

   ii. There are several data types; not all data types fit for all situations.

   iii. Data abstractions manage complexity in programs— variable names, for example, help in the following way:

      ▸ you do not need to know how the variable is stored or even the values within the variable to use it in a program.

      ▸ variable names can contain different types of elements including lists.

EXAMPLE 1:

Matching: Column I holds data types. Column II holds data you are trying to store. Match the data type to the data.

Column I: Data Types	Column II: Data Description
A. Number	1. a person's name
B. String	2. three questions to be used in a quiz
C. List	3. the cost of an item

Answer: A3, B1, C2

A (Number) matches to 3 (cost) because the cost of an item would be stored as a number. A good name for this number might be price. B (String) matches to 1 (name) because a person's name would most likely be stored as a string. A good name for this string might be name. C (List) matches to 2 (quiz questions) because lists hold groups of items, like three questions. A good name for this list might be questions.

B. The way statements are ordered and combined determines what the program does.

1. Ways to control execution of code:

   i.   sequence: code executes line-by-line

   ii. selection: conditions being true or false control which lines of code are executed

   iii. iteration: looping causes lines of code to be repeated for a certain number of times or until a condition is met

2. Statements often respond to data being modified or events (like button clicks) in a program.

3. Relational operators and logical operators return Boolean results (true or false) and these results help control execution of code.

   i.   Relational operators: =, ≠, <, ≤, >, and ≥

   ii. Logical operators: AND, OR, NOT

4. The order of conditional statements can lead to the same meaning as a logical operator.

   i.   Two nested IF's are equivalent to AND

IF A
   IF B
      `<statement>`
	IS LOGICALLY EQUIVALENT TO:	IF (A AND B)
		  `<statement>`

   ii. An IF followed by an ELSE IF is equivalent to OR

IF A
    `<statement>`
ELSE
  IF B
   `<statement>`
	IS LOGICALLY EQUIVALENT TO:	IF (A OR B)
		  `<statement>`

C. Creating new algorithms requires planning and practice.

1. Knowledge of existing algorithms can help you to create new algorithms.

2. There are many ways to write an algorithm that does what it is supposed to do.

   i.   You should write code sequences to be as clear as possible to other people who are reading your code.

   ii. Choose variable names and logical statements that are clear.

   iii. Follow conventions of the programming language you are using.

3. Order of Operations:

   i.   When you are handling questions on the End-of-Course Exam, assume that the order of operations used in mathematics applies when you evaluate expressions.

   ▸ Parentheses

   ▸ Exponents

   ▸ Multiplication (*), Division (/), or Modulus (MOD), whatever comes first from left to right

   ▸ Addition (+) or Subtraction (–), whatever comes first from left to right

   ▸ Assignment happens last. Assignment only happens after the arithmetic operations occur to the right of the assignment operator.

   ii. This order is the same as the order you would have practiced in math classes.

Test Tip

The nuances of the End-of-Course Exam pseudocode as well as some practice examples are in Chapter 13 of your Crash Course. *If you have not already read that chapter, you should go back and read it. In addition, check out the Exam Reference Sheet provided in Appendix E.*

EXAMPLE 2:

Find x if x ← 10 – 7 MOD 3 * 2

Answer: 8

The steps are as follows:

STEP 1: Modulus first: Since 7 MOD 3 = 1, 10 – **7 MOD 3** * 2 = 10 – **1** * 2

STEP 2: Multiplication: Since 1*2 = 2, 10 – **1 * 2** = 10 – 2

STEP 3: Subtraction: 10 – 2 = 8

D. Procedures

1. Procedures can take zero or more arguments.

2. Procedures can return a value to be stored in a variable.

3. Return statements mean flow of control is returned to where the procedure was called.

4. Strategies to create and use procedures:

    i.   Remove shared features and/or use parameters to generalize functionality instead of duplicating code.

    ii. Write procedures that have removed shared features and/or use parameters to allow for program code reuse, helping to manage complexity.

         ▸ Improves code readability because all the lines of code necessary for a procedure are replaced with a procedure name that calls these lines.

         ▸ Allows programmers to improve the procedure without needing to notify users of the change as long as the procedure still operates as intended.

5. Programmers often break down problems into smaller pieces and use procedures to manage these pieces.

    i.   Called "Procedural Abstraction"

▸ A programmer should only need to know a procedure's name, inputs, and behavior to decide whether they want to use it or not.

▸ A programmer does not necessarily need to know how the procedure works.

▸ In this way, procedures help programmers manage complexity.

ii. Software libraries exist to help programmers know the procedures that come along with a programming language.

▸ Libraries can be internal or external.

– Internal library: already existing code that was created by you or other programmers in your environment.

– External library: code created by language developers or people not in your normal coding environment.

iii. Application Program Interfaces (API's) – documentation explaining what each procedure expects for input, the behavior of the procedure, and what, if anything, the procedure will return.

▸ Internal documentation could be comments in your code or a reference document created and shared with other coders in your environment.

▸ External documentation can often be found via a search engine for the programming language you are using.

▸ Documentation is necessary to understand available procedures and how to use them.

6. An example of a typical procedure that comes with a programming language is one that simulates randomness.

i. You will need to write and analyze code that uses randomness to simulate real random events.

      ii.   You will need to decide how to use randomness to correctly model a situation being described.

   7. Simulations are another form of abstraction.

      i.   More complex objects or problems are simulated using computer programs to help the programmer or user focus on key details that matter to them.

      ii.   Simulations often mimic real-world events so that users of the simulation can make conclusions or investigate something without the constraints or consequences of the real world.

      iii.   Simulations can contain bias based on the details that are included or excluded from the simulation.

      iv.   Random number generators can be used to simulate random events.

      v.   Simulations are ideal tools if a real-world event cannot be created easily.

E. Exceptions

   1. Not all solutions are equally efficient.

      i.   Optimization problems (like the traveling salesperson) tend to run in an unreasonable amount of time unless a heuristic is applied.

         ▶ These algorithms tend to have exponential (or worse, factorial) efficiencies.

         ▶ These are the algorithms where a heuristic can be helpful.

      ii.   Algorithms that have polynomial efficiency or faster are said to run in reasonable time.

      iii.   You can determine efficiency through formal mathematical reasoning.

      iv.   You can approximate efficiency by measuring the amount of times a statement or group of statements executes.

2. There are problems that computers cannot solve and even when a computer can solve a problem, it may not be able to do so in a reasonable amount of time.

3. The following table is created to provide a list of common algorithms and their efficiency. More details on some of these algorithms are provided later in this chapter.

Name of Algorithm	Run in Reasonable Time?	What Algorithm Does	Efficiency	Approximate number of comparisons for n items
Binary Search	YES	Look at the middle of an ordered set. If the target is less than the number in the middle, remove the top half of the set. If the target is greater than the number in the middle, remove the bottom half of the set. Repeat until the target is found or there are no more elements.	Logarithmic	$\log_2(n)$ (however, the target could be in the middle position and found in the first loop)
Linear Search	YES	Look at each element in a set, one at a time, until you find the target or you reach the end of the set.	Linear	n (however, the target could be in the first position and found in the first loop)
Find the minimum of a set	YES	Initialize minimum to be the first element in the set. Compare the current minimum to each element and if current element is smaller than the current minimum, the minimum is assigned to that element.	Linear	n (minimum could be the last item in the list, have to consider all)

(continued)

Name of Algorithm	Run in Reasonable Time?	What Algorithm Does	Efficiency	Approximate number of comparisons for n items
Find the maximum of a set	YES	Initialize maximum to be the first element in the set. Compares the maximum to each element and if current element is larger than the current maximum, the maximum is assigned to that element.	Linear	n (maximum could be the last item in the list, have to consider all)
Find the sum of a set of numbers	YES	Initializes a sum variable to 0. For each element in the set, add the sum to that element. Continue until the end of the set is reached.	Linear	n (have to sum all elements in the list)
Find the average of a set of numbers	YES	Create the loop to calculate the sum. Divide the sum by the total number of elements in the set.	Linear	n (have to sum all elements in the list)
Sorting Algorithms	YES	Examples: Radix, Selection, Bubble, Merge, Quick	Linear to Quadratic	Between n and n^2 (depends on the sorting algorithm)
Larger Optimization Problems	NO	Examples: Traveling Salesperson, Find Least Amount of Materials, Find the Shortest Path	Exponential or Factorial	2^n to n! (depends on the algorithm and situation)

The table above is ordered from most efficient to least efficient. Only larger optimization problems (see the last row) tend to run in an unreasonable amount of time for larger data sets.

To understand why a polynomial number of comparisons is considered reasonable time and exponential or factorial are not, consider what happens to n^2 and 2^n as n increases in size. When n=2, the difference is not clear. In fact, $n^2 = 2^n$. To see why 2^n is generally larger than n^2, you need to consider larger numbers. So, let's consider n=10. $n^2 = 10^2 = 100$ and $2^n = 2^{10} = 1024$. The number of comparisons required is much more for 2^n when compared to n^2 as n increases. This would be true for any positive integer. If you were to compare n^3 to 3^n, as n increases, 3^n would be much larger than n^3. Now, if you compare all of these to a factorial, you would see why n! is considered even more inefficient. $10! = 3,628,800$. So, in general, you can assume that as n increases, for any constant k, $n^k < k^n < n!$. This is why algorithms that have exponential or worse efficiencies often require a heuristic to have a chance at reaching a solution.

V. WHAT YOU NEED TO BE ABLE TO DO WITH ALGORITHMS AND PROGRAMMING

A. You need to be able to write, analyze, and debug code for standard algorithms.

1. Finding the minimum of a list involves the following:

    i.   two data structures: a list and a variable to hold the minimum when found;

    ii. a loop to access each element in the list.

    iii. The pseudocode for finding the minimum of a list is:

```
min = list[1]
for each item in list
    if item < min
        min = item
return min
```

2. Finding the maximum of a list involves the following:

   i. two data structures and a loop

   ii. The pseudocode for finding the maximum will look like the following:

   ```
   max = list[1]
   for each item in list
       if item > max
           max = item
   return max
   ```

3. Finding the sum of numbers in a list involves the following:

   i. two data structures: a list and a variable to hold the sum when calculated

   ii. a loop to get to each item in the list

   iii. Pseudocode for finding the sum might look like the following:

   ```
   sum = 0
   for each item in list
       sum = item + sum
   return sum
   ```

4. Finding the average of a list of numbers involves the following:

   i. three data structures: a list and two variables to hold the sum

   ii. the average when calculated

   iii. a loop to get to each item in the list

   iv. To calculate the average, you need the sum. Here is possible pseudocode for average:

   ```
   average = 0
   sum = 0
   for each item in list
       sum = item + sum
   if (length of list) ≥ 1
       average = sum /(length of list)
   return average
   ```

Note that in the algorithm for average, the IF statement checks that there is at least one element in the list before dividing. This prevents division by 0. If there is no element in the list, this algorithm would return 0 as the average.

5. Searching for an element (often called a "target") in a list involves the following:

   i. two data structures: a list and a variable to hold the location if found

   ii. a loop to get to each item in the list

   iii. There are two algorithms for finding a target that you need to know:

   ▸ linear search

   ▸ binary search

B. Know the difference between linear (sequential) search and binary search. (These are the two types of search algorithms you will see on the test.)

   1. Both linear and binary searches try to find an element in a list.

   2. Linear search starts with the first element, looks at each element one at a time to see if it is the correct element, and if it is, returns the location.

   3. Binary search starts with the middle element of a sorted list, compares the target to that middle element, removes the half of the set where the target is not located, and continues until the target is found or no more elements remain.

   4. Each search algorithm has its advantages and drawbacks:

   i. Linear search is much easier to code, but is less efficient for larger sets.

   ii. Binary search only works on ordered sets, but it is more efficient for larger sets.

For the multiple-choice programming languages, the first element in a list is 1 and the last element in a list is equal to the length of the list. This may be different from the language that you are learning. Since this section is to help you get ready for the multiple-choice test, this is the approach you will see here to iterate through a list. Assume list[index] is the element in list at index and a return of –1 means that the target was not found.

5. Linear Search

   i. Pseudocode for linear search might look something like this:

   STEP 1: Ask person what they are trying to find.
   STEP 2: Store this in a variable called TARGET.
   STEP 3: Create and store 0 in a variable called index.
   STEP 4: While index < length of list
         index = index + 1
         Compare TARGET to list[index]
           If TARGET = element
             return index
           else
             index = index + 1
   STEP 5: return –1

   ▸ So if a list has 10 elements, the search will take at most 10 loops to determine if the target is in the list, or not.

   ▸ Note that there are no special requirements on the list to make linear search work. This is one way that linear search is different from binary search.

6. Binary Search

   i. Binary search assumes that a list is already in order and takes advantage of this.

   ii. Binary search is called "binary" because it repeatedly splits the list into two parts.

   iii. After each loop of this search, half the list is removed.

iv. For each division by 2, if the result is not an integer, you can assume that it rounds up. The procedure that manages this is not shown. It is called roundup.

v. Pseudocode for binary search might look something like this (You can assume that if the target is not found, the code should return –1.):

STEP 1: Ask person what they are trying to find.
STEP 2: Store this in a variable called TARGET.
STEP 3: Create variables called low, high, and middle.
STEP 4: low = 1
STEP 5: high = length of list
STEP 6: middle = roundUp((length of list)/2)
STEP 7: While (low ≤ high)
      if (list[middle] < TARGET)
         low = middle
      else if (list[middle] > TARGET)
         high = middle
      else if (list[middle]=TARGET)
         return middle
      middle = roundUp((low + high)/2)
STEP 8: return –1

vi. Notice that this algorithm is more complicated to code.

Test Tip

You do not need to worry about writing search algorithms from scratch. It is important to notice why the list needs to be ordered for binary search to work. It is important for you to notice that these algorithms have different efficiencies. Linear search is linear. Binary search is logarithmic.

vii. Let's trace it through with the following short list of alphabetized items:

▸ Assume that the list we are searching is:

▸ {"ANT", "BAT", "CAT", "DOG", "HORSE", "LION"}

▸ Our target (the element we want to find) is "DOG"

▸ Stepping through the code, low = 1, high = 6, and middle = $\frac{6}{2}$ = 3.

- ▸ Since low < high, we enter the *while* loop.
  - – list[middle] = list[3] = "CAT"
  - – Since "CAT" < "DOG", the first if statement is true. So low = 3.
  - – middle = roundUp$\left(\dfrac{(3+6)}{2}\right)$ = roundUp(4.5) = 5
  - – high is still 6
  - – Notice how the list is now split in half.
    - a. The new low is 3. The new high is 6
    - b. Since "DOG" cannot be in a position less than 3, we will not look at that lower half of the set again.
    - c. Half of the set is eliminated in one loop!
- ▸ Back to the while loop: low(3) is still less than high(6) so we loop again
  - – list[middle] = list[5] = "HORSE"
  - – This time, "HORSE" > "DOG" so the *else if* statement is true.
    - a. This time, high is modified to 5 and low remains at 3.
    - b. Once again, the set is split in half and this time, the lower half remains
    - c. After the *else if* ends, middle = roundUp$\left(\dfrac{(3+5)}{2}\right)$ = 4
  - – Again, we enter the *while* loop since low(3) is less than high(5)
    - a. list[middle] = list[4] = "DOG"
    - b. Since the third *else if* will be true, the procedure will return middle, which is 4.
- ▸ Note that it took three loops to locate "DOG". In a sequential search, it would have taken four loops.

Try tracing the search for a different target. Tracing code or pseudocode takes practice. The more examples you do ahead of the multiple-choice exam, the more likely you will find an approach to tracing that works for you.

viii. Usually, in an ordered set, binary search is faster than a linear search.

  ‣ On average, if the set has 16 elements, it would take 4 loops to find the target.

    – Can you see why? Each loop eliminates half the set. So 16 elements would go to 8 elements in loop 1, 4 elements in loop 2, 2 elements in loop 3, and find the target in loop 4.

  ‣ Binary search would take about 5 loops for 32 elements, 6 loops for 64, and so on.

  ‣ For *n* elements, binary search will take $\log_2 n$ loops to find the target.

  ‣ In an ordered set, the larger *n* gets, the larger the advantage of using binary search instead of linear search:

Size of set	Number of loops in Linear Search	Number of loops in Binary Search
8	8	3
64	64	6
256	256	8
n	N	$\log_2(n)$

EXAMPLE 3 (SNEAK PEEK):

A list called dogs contains the names of dogs found in a park. A person wants to write a procedure to return the location if the dog name is in dogs and –1 if the dog name is not in dogs.

The person has the following procedures available to create this new procedure called findDog:

Procedure	Explanation
sort(list)	Sorts list in alphabetical order and returns the resulting list
binarySearch(target, list)	Performs a binary search to return the location of target in list if target is in the list, –1 otherwise
linearSearch(target, list)	Performs a linear search to return the location of target in list if target is in list, –1 otherwise

The procedure will look like THIS:

```
PROCEDURE findDog(name, dogs)
{
   <instructions>
   RETURN (location)
}
```

Which of the following could NOT replace <instructions> to correctly implement this procedure?

(A) location = linearSearch(name, sort(dogs))

(B) location = binarySearch(name, dogs)

(C) location = binarySearch(name, sort(dogs))

(D) location = linearSearch(name, dogs)

Answer: (B)

Binary search requires that the list is sorted. Choice (B) calls `binarySearch` without first sorting the list, so it would not correctly implement the procedure. Linear search has no such requirement. Whether a list is sorted or not, the linear search algorithm looks at all elements in a list so either Choice (A) or (D) would find the target correctly. Choice (C) correctly sorts before attempting binary search.

C. You need to be able to determine the result of code segments written using sequence, selection, and/or iteration.

D. You need to be able to express a coding solution without using a programming language—for example, by using a flowchart, words, or pseudocode.

E. You need to be able to explain that variables, lists, and procedures are all abstractions helping you manage complexity as you program.

F. You need to be able to write and evaluate expressions using relational and logical operators.

G. You need to recognize when you are reading about a situation where a heuristic may be a part of the solution.

1. Heuristics help an algorithm that is not running in reasonable time to reach a solution, even if it is not the optimal solution.

2. Larger optimization problems normally require a heuristic to run in reasonable time.

H. You need to be able to explain that not all problems are decidable in computer science.

1. An undecidable problem may have a solution for some situations, but not all.

2. A decidable problem has a solution for all situations.

3. Therefore, a decidable problem may or may not run in reasonable time, but could be solvable.

4. An undecidable problem may or may not run in reasonable time and it may or may not be solvable.

I. You need to be able to use smaller procedures to build larger procedures.

J. You need to consider how to use programming to connect to real-world situations.

EXAMPLE 4 (SNEAK PEEK):

Suppose you would like to create a procedure to find and print the smallest item in the list. The procedure might look like this:

```
PROCEDURE printMin(theList)
{
  min ← 0
  FOR EACH item IN theList
  {
    if (min > item)
    {
      min ← item
    }
  }
  DISPLAY ("smallest item in list is " + min)
}
```

In what situation would this procedure fail to correctly display the minimum?

(A) In no situation; this procedure works as intended.

(B) In all situations; this procedure will display the maximum, not the minimum.

(C) If every item in the list is positive

(D) If every item in the list is negative

Answer: (C)

Choice (C) is correct because if every item is positive, then the condition "min>item" will never be `true`. The min will remain set to 0. To avoid this, when finding the minimum, the test variable (min for this example) should be set to the maximum allowable value in your programming language. Alternatively, you could set it to an element of the list.

EXAMPLE 5 (SNEAK PEEK):

Which of the following algorithms, given a list of integers, require both selection and iteration?

(A) An algorithm that swaps the first and last elements of the list.

(B) An algorithm that calculates the sum of the elements in the list.

(C) An algorithm that returns true if the first element equals the second.

(D) An algorithm that returns the number of elements that are positive.

Answer: (D)

Choice (A) is not correct because swapping requires the creation of a third variable, not iteration. Choice (B) is incorrect because finding the sum of a list does not require selection, since the entire list will be summed. Choice (C) is incorrect because testing for equality is a conditional statement, not iteration. The only algorithm that requires both selection and iteration is Choice (D) since you need to use a conditional to test if the number is positive, and iteration to access all members of the list.

EXAMPLE 6 (SNEAK PEEK):

A sales representative has a list of clients to visit. All clients live in different cities and each client should be visited exactly once. Which question would be most likely to require a heuristic in order to make a decision in reasonable time?

(A) What is the shortest route the representative can take?

(B) After the route is complete, what is the maximum sale amount?

(C) Using last year's results to predict, what is the expected total sales this year?

(D) After sorting the sales by city, in which city was the largest sale?

Answer: (A)

Choice (A) is correct because this is an optimization problem called the traveling salesperson problem. Optimization problems are most likely to require heuristics, especially for a large number of cities. Choices (B), (C), and (D) are solvable without a heuristic.

EXAMPLE 7 (SNEAK PEEK):

Consider the following procedure intended to print the odd integers from 1 up to *n*. The procedure does not work as intended.

```
Line 1:   PROCEDURE printOdds(n)
Line 2:   {
Line 3:      num ← 0
Line 4:      REPEAT UNTIL (num ≥ n)
Line 5:      {
Line 6:         num ← num + 1
Line 7:         if ((num / 2) ≠ 0)
Line 8:         {
Line 9:            print (num)
Line 10:        }
Line 11:     }
Line 12: }
```

Which of the following changes can be made so that the procedure will work as intended?

(A) Changing line 3 to num ← 1

(B) Changing line 4 to REPEAT UNTIL (num ≤ n)

(C) Moving line 6 so it is between lines 10 and 11

(D) Changing line 7 to if ((num MOD 2) ≠ 0)

Answer: (D)

Choice (D) is correct because if ((num / 2) ≠ 0) would cause num to be printed several times it should not print. For example, if num were 2, if ((num / 2) ≠ 0) would be true and num would print, even though 2 is not odd. Changing this statement to if ((num MOD 2) ≠ 0) would mean that num would only print if the division remainder of num/2 was not 0. This would only happen when num is odd. Choice (A) is not correct because changing line 3 to num ← 1 would not impact what is printed. Choice (B) is not correct because this would mean the loop would never begin. Num < n at the start of the program, so the REPEAT condition would already be reached and no code inside the REPEAT would run. Choice (C) is not correct because this would not impact the code's performance, whether n is odd or even.

Let's trace for *n* = 2, where 1 should be printed:

num before REPEAT	(num ≥ n)	num before corrected Line 7, if ((num MOD 2) ≠ 0)	What is printed?
0	false	1	1
1	false	2	
2	true	Loop does not execute, nothing is printed	

Let's trace for *n* = 3, where 1 and 3 should be printed:

num before REPEAT	(num ≥ n)	num before corrected Line 7, if ((num MOD 2) ≠ 0)	What is printed?
0	false	1	1
1	false	2	
2	false	3	3
3	true	Loop does not execute, nothing is printed	

Test Tip

Questions from this topic are the most common questions you will see on your End-of-Course Exam. Twenty-one to 25 of the 70 questions focus on this topic! Ultimately, the best way to learn how to trace, debug, and analyze code is to write programs. Look for ideas that challenge you to do new things in the language you are learning.

Big Idea 4: Computer Systems & Networks

I. OVERVIEW

A. About 11%–15% of the End-of-Course Exam questions will focus on Computer Systems and Networks.

B. This means you can expect 8–11 questions out of 70 to be focused on this topic.

II. WHAT ARE COMPUTER SYSTEMS AND NETWORKS?

A. Computer Systems and Networks are wired and wireless connections between devices created to allow devices to share data.

B. The largest and most popular network of devices is the internet.

III. QUESTIONS YOU CAN ASK YOURSELF THROUGHOUT THE YEAR THAT ARE RELATED TO THIS TOPIC:

A. What are the benefits of dividing tasks among group members? Is there a point where adding another group member would not help? Why?

B. What does redundancy and fault-tolerance have to do with the internet?

C. When a system is scalable, what does this mean?

D. How am I able to communicate to a family member on the internet?

 IV. WHAT YOU NEED TO KNOW ABOUT COMPUTER SYSTEMS AND NETWORKS

A. Related to Computing Devices and Networks

- computing device—physical device that can run a program; examples: computer, tablet, server, router, smart sensor

- computing system—group of connected devices and programs working together for a common purpose

- computer network—type of computing system capable of sending or receiving data

- path—sequence of directly connected computing devices beginning at the sender and ending at the receiver

- routing—finding a path from sender to receiver

- bandwidth—maximum amount of data that can be sent in a fixed amount of time; measured in bits per second

B. Related to How the Internet Works

- protocol—agreed upon rules that specify behavior in system; common internet protocols are HTTP (HyperText Transfer Protocol), IP (Internet Protocol), TCP (Transmission Control Protocol), and UDP (User Datagram Protocol).

- scalability (of a system) – the ability of the system to change in size and scale to meet new demands

- data stream—expression for the way information is passed through the internet; data streams contain organized chunks of data called packets

- World Wide Web—system of linked pages, programs, and files that uses the internet to provide you with access to it

C. Related to Fault-Tolerance

▸ redundancy—inclusion of extra components to prevent failure of the system if a component fails

▸ fault-tolerant—when a system can support failures and still continue to function

D. Related to Parallel and Distributed Computing

▸ sequential computing—operations are performed in order, one at a time

▸ parallel computing—operations are broken into smaller parts, some of which are performed simultaneously

▸ distributed computing—multiple devices are being used to run a program

▸ efficiency—measured and compared using time to complete tasks

V. WHAT YOU NEED TO UNDERSTAND ABOUT COMPUTER SYSTEMS AND NETWORKS

A. Computer Systems and Networks are used to move and store data.

1. Data transfer and processing is impacted by the amount of processing power available.

   i. If you are using one computer, transferring and processing information can be slow.

   ii. Using multiple computers to do different parts of a process at the same time can significantly shorten the time required to complete tasks or solve problems.

2. The internet is the largest and most commonly used network.

   i. Using a series of protocols, the internet allows people and devices to send and receive information throughout the world.

      ii.   These protocols are open, allowing users to easily connect new devices to the internet.

B. The internet is not the same as the World Wide Web.

    1. The World Wide Web is a system of linked pages, programs, and files.

      i.   We use the World Wide Web to access the internet.

      ii.   HTTP is a protocol used by the World Wide Web.

    2. The internet is a worldwide network of billions of computers and other electronic devices.

C. Data flows across a network from one device to another. The OSI Model is a theoretical model to help understand how this works.

Test Tip

The OSI Model is a convenient way to organize much of the information that is covered on your exam. Do not get caught up in the details. Instead, look at the OSI Model as a way to see software, hardware, and protocols as interconnected concepts that support communication from one device to another across a network.

    1. There are seven layers in the OSI Model.

      i.   Layer 1 (Physical) is about the cables and other physical connections that support connectivity.

      ii.   Layer 2 (Data Link) is where Media Access Control (MAC) addresses are found. MAC addresses are unique addresses given to hardware on a network.

      iii.   Layer 3 (Network) is where IP address routing decisions are being made.

      iv.   Layer 4 (Transport) is part of IP communication. It is where transportation protocols (UDP or User Datagram

Protocol and TCP or Transmission Control Protocol) are managed.

v. Layer 5 (Session) is where control protocols to start and stop application sessions will occur.

vi. Layer 6 (Presentation) handles information that will be encrypted and decrypted.

vii. Layer 7 (Application) is the layer we see as we use a web application.

Test Tip

You will never be asked about these layers or the OSI model. It is here because it is a good way to organize most of the "Computer Systems and Networks" information that you will be asked about on your End-of-Course Exam.

2. Sending information across a network often involves all 7 layers as follows:

Layer 7: Application
Layer 6: Presentation
Layer 5: Session
Layer 4: Transport
Layer 3: Network
Layer 2: Data Link
Layer 1: Physical

i. Everything begins and ends with the physical layer or Layer 1.

▸ This layer represents the signal that is transporting our information across the network and the hardware and cables that carry that signal.

▸ Protocols are not really a factor in this layer; it is about cables and other necessary physical devices.

ii. Layer 2 is the data link layer.

▸ This layer is about switching and/ or having two devices communicate with each other.

▸ You can think of this layer as having data link control protocols. On an Ethernet network, MAC (hardware) addresses are how devices find each other.

  iii. Layer 3 is the network layer.

    ▸ This layer is also called the routing layer. It is responsible for breaking data into appropriately sized packets for the network to be able to process.

    ▸ This is an Internet Protocol layer. IP addresses are used.

  iv. Layer 4 is the transport layer.

    ▸ Some people also call this the "post office layer" because it is here that packets are transported to their destinations.

    ▸ Key protocols:

     – UDP = User Datagram Protocol

     – TCP = Transmission Control Protocol

  v. Layer 5 is the session layer, controlling the starting and stopping of applications.

  vi. Layer 6 is the presentation layer.

    ▸ This layer is focused on character encoding and application encryption.

    ▸ An example of a protocol used in this layer is SSL/TLS (Secure Socket Layer/Transport Layer Security) protocol.

  vii. Layer 7 is the application layer.

    ▸ This is what we can see. It may be a browser window, our email, or a file.

    ▸ HTTP (HyperText Transfer Protocol) is used in Layer 7.

D. The OSI Model should help you understand:

 1. Communication from one location on a network to another involves layers of protocols to support that communication.

  i. These layers also provide a way to describe and diagnose problems in that communication.

ii. The layers that are the focus for the End-of-Course Exam are:

> ▸ Layer 3 (routing or network layer)
>
> ▸ Layer 4 (transport or "post office" layer)
>
> ▸ Layer 6 (presentation layer)
>
> ▸ Layer 7 (application layer)

Test Tip

You DO NOT need to know these layers by name. The names are here to give some organization and context to what you do need to know in a way that also makes sense to industry professionals.

E. Suppose you have information that you want to send across a network to a friend. Here are the steps to explain how this works and how this is connected to the OSI Model:

STEP 1: Before any transmission can be successful, both you and your friend had to connect to this network.

i. Your device and your friend's device were each assigned IP addresses.

ii. Look at IP addresses like your mailing address. They give your device a way to be found on the network.

STEP 2: The information (the email and the image, for example) is broken into small pieces for the network to be able to process.

i. This happens in Layer 3, the network or routing layer.

ii. Internet Protocol uses IP addresses to send the information from your device location on the network to your friend's device.

iii. These small pieces of information are called "IP packets."

iv. In addition to the data itself, packets contain the following key information to help them get to their destination:

▸ their source (IP address that they came from)

▸ destination (IP address that they are trying to reach)

STEP 3: Depending on the type of information you are sending and the type of network you are using, some information will be sent using UDP (User Datagram Protocol) or TCP (Transmission Control Protocol).

i. This decision happens in Layer 4, the transport or "post office" layer.

ii. As packets are moving across a network, many things can happen to them.

▸ They may be lost.

▸ They may be re-routed to other locations on the way to their final destination IP address.

▸ They may be dropped because it took too long for them to arrive.

iii. Depending on the type of protocol being used, what has happened to packets may or may not be known or fixable.

▸ If TCP (Transmission Control Protocol) is used, packets that are lost or dropped can be re-requested.

   – TCP is "connection-oriented," meaning two devices are connected, information is exchanged, then the connection is ended.

   – TCP packets contain extra information to allow themselves to be tracked and to be re-requested if they are lost or dropped.

   – When a packet is received at its destination, there is acknowledgement that the information was received.

   – This means that TCP packets are more likely to get from their source to their destination, but they may take longer and require more bandwidth to get there.

▸ If UDP (User Datagram Protocol) is used, packets that are lost or dropped are not re-requested.

  – UDP is considered "connectionless" – if data is available, UDP will start sending it, whether or not a device is ready to receive.

  – If data is lost, this would not be known by the sender or receiver so there is no way to recover that lost data.

  – UDP packets have less information than TCP packets so they require less bandwidth and can arrive faster.

▸ Use a traceroute tool to see layers 3 and 4 "in action." There is an online version here: *uptrends. com/tools/traceroute.*

▸ Type the website address you are trying to reach and notice that the IP addresses used along the way are shown to you.

▸ Test this address again and notice that the pathway and times may be different.

Test Tip

Notice how TCP is more fault-tolerant because it has more redundancies built into it. These redundancies come with more overhead (time and processing requirements), but some applications accept these extras in exchange for increased reliability.

STEP 4: Your friend's device receives the packets, which are reassembled so your friend can read your message and view the image.

  i. This is a combination of Layers 5 (session) and 6 (presentation).

  ii. When the packets are received on your friend's side of the network, your friend will want to choose an appropriate application to interact with this information, and any encrypted messages are decrypted so they can be read.

   iii. A protocol that really matters in this layer is SSL/ TLS (Secure Socket Layer / Transport Layer Security) protocol, which manages:

- character encoding
- application encryption and decryption

STEP 5: Your friend is able to view what you sent to them in their browser.

   i. This is a Layer 7 or application-layer behavior.

   ii. In this layer, HTTP (Hypertext Transfer Protocol) allows your friend to locate where the reassembled files are stored and view them.

 VI. **IDEAS RELATED TO BANDWIDTH AND REDUNDANCY**

A. Not all information is sent across a network with the same speed.

1. Bandwidth measures the bits per second that can be transmitted across a network.

2. Most of the time, bandwidth advertised by an Internet Service Provider will be higher than your actual internet speed.

3. Here are some of the things that might impact the speed of the internet in your school or home:

   i. the number of devices you are using

   ii. firewalls

   iii. whether or not you are using an updated router

4. Test your bandwidth at school or at home by going to *speedtest.net*.

    i.   Hit "GO" to see the amount of data per second you are currently downloading from and uploading to the internet.

    ii. You should notice your bandwidth decreases when more devices in your household are connected. This is similar to traffic slowing down on a highway when many people are trying to use it at once.

B. Not all information sent across a network is received.

   1. Redundancies are built into networks to improve the likelihood that information will be received.

   2. The more routes available for data to be sent from one location in a network to another, the more redundant that network is.

   3. Creating more pathways means more resources to build those physical connections, but more redundancy also means a more fault tolerant system.

Test Tip

While redundancy in a system often requires additional resources, it can provide the added benefit of fault tolerance. This is a key concept in your End-of-Course Exam.

VII. IDEAS RELATED TO SCALABILITY

A. If a network was suddenly so flooded with traffic that the packets could not reach their destination, more connections and pathways would need to be built.

B. Scalability is the extent to which a system can grow to accommodate new needs.

C. The internet was designed to be scalable. One example is IPv4 being widened to IPv6.

  1. IPv4 addresses consist of 4 bytes or 32 bits.

    i. Here is an example of an IPv4 address: 192.168.3.131

▸ Converted to binary, so we see it the way a computer would "see" it:

    11000000.10101000.00000011.10000011

▸ In binary, you can see the 32 bits clearly.

▸ At most, IPv4 can accommodate 2^{32} addresses ranging from the smallest possible address: 0.0.0.0 to the largest possible address 255.255.255.255.

  – If all 8 billion people in the world wanted to connect with a unique IP address, there would not be enough IP addresses for each person.

  – $\dfrac{2^{32}\ \text{addresses}}{8{,}000{,}000{,}000\ \text{people}} \approx 0.5$ or approximately ½ an address per person

  – Most people want to connect more than one device (smartphone, computer, etc.).

Test Tip

Did you try the binary conversion yourself? You should! From Chapter 15, you know converting from decimal to binary and binary to decimal is a skill you need to practice. Take advantage of this time and practice.

    ii. IPv6 addresses provide more addresses to people and their devices.

▸ Instead of 32 bits, IPv6 addresses have 128 bits.

▸ This would allow each of the approximately 8 billion people in the world to have 40 octillion (4.0×10^{28}) addresses each.

   iii. The fact that IP addresses and the rules they need to follow are publicly available have helped to make this system scalable.

It is important to do something with what you are learning. It will help you to remember information you are learning and it is a lot more fun. To see your IPv4 and IPv6 address, go to whatismyipaddress.com. For extra fun, see if you can figure out what your IPv4 address would look like in binary; then check your solution.

D. Another example of the scalability of the internet is the (DNS) domain name system.

   1. Anytime you are typing an address like "rea.com", that address needs to be converted to an IP address.

   i. You only need to remember "rea.com".

   ii. DNS handles that conversion.

   2. DNS is hierarchical.

   i. DNS is a structure with levels, each with a specific purpose.

   ii. It follows a specific path to find exactly the server you are trying to locate.

   3. DNS is an example of a distributed database with many DNS servers throughout the world.

   i. There are hundreds of generic top-level domains (gTDLs) like .com, .edu, .org, etc.

   ii. TDLs and subdomains can be added as needed to satisfy demand.

4. Here is an example of the hierarchy of DNS:

```
                          ( . )
                           |
        +------------------+------------------+
        |                  |                  |
     (.com)             (.edu)             (.net)
        |
  (yourWebsite)
        |
  +-----------+-----------+-----------+
  |           |           |           |
(www)      (mail)      (east)      (west)
                           |           |
                      +----+----+  +---+----+
                      |         |  |        |
                   (bella)  (dave)(carol)(bill)
```

i.   Using the internet, we often see ".com" or ".net", which are examples of top-level domains.

ii. When people purchase domain names, they also need to decide on at least one top-level domain.

   ▸ Suppose you purchase the domain name, "yourWebsite" and you chose ".com" for your top level domain.

   ▸ So the address would be: yourWebsite.com.

   ▸ At "yourWebsite," there may be a web server named "www."

      – The web server is the computer system that will deliver web pages to clients.

      – It would be named: "www.yourWebsite.com"

   ▸ You may also have other locations under yourWebsite called mail, east, or west.

      – We can specify the fully qualified domain name for each.

      – For example, mail's domain on yourWebsite.com is "mail.yourWebsite.com".

▸ Finally, you may have servers that are one level down from that. So bella is located on east.yourWebsite.com or, using the fully qualified domain name: bella.east.yourWebsite.com.

▸ Notice how you can enlarge your domain as needed by adding subdomains and files as long as you follow this structure.

In a system that is scalable, it can grow in size without sacrificing much by way of integrity or performance. Notice that as the internet has grown, the domain name system has scaled to support this growth. New domains have been added, new applications to support users have been created, but the system has remained intact. This is why DNS is considered scalable.

iii. The following image will help you picture what this looks like in connected form.

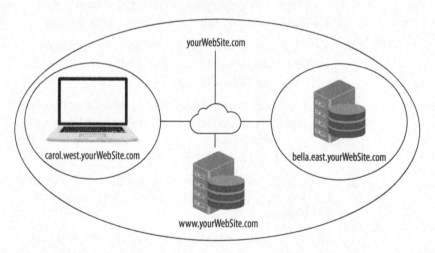

VIII. **IDEAS RELATED TO DISTRIBUTED COMPUTING**

A. A distributed system is a system with many components (software and hardware) located in different locations that communicate and coordinate with each other.

1. There are many examples of distributed systems on the internet.

2. Distributed systems coordinate so well that people using them often do not know that they are distributed because they appear to be working as well as a non-distributed system.

B. The Domain Name System (DNS) is a very distributed database.

1. A distributed database is a database that is not located in one location, but instead in many locations across the internet.

2. To find all of the services that are located as fully qualified domain names, we may need to ask many servers.

3. Starting with a laptop (could be a smartphone or a personal computer), the device will try to find the IP address associated with www.yourWebsite.com.

   i. Your laptop is configured with a Local Name Server that it will reference to see if it can find the IP address.

      ‣ Your laptop will "query" (means "ask", in database language) that database, "What is the IP address for www.yourWebsite.com"?

      ‣ The Local Name Server keeps a record of the places you have been before and if you had been to www.yourWebsite.com, it would provide the IP address using this record called a "cache."

   ii. If the Local Name Server does not have the IP address for yourWebsite.com in its cache, it then queries the Root Server.

   iii. The Root Server responds back to the Local Name Server instructing it to look to the ".com Name Server" because the top-level domain in www.yourWebsite.com is ".com".

   iv. The Local Name Server does as it is told and asks the .com Name Server whether that server knows the IP address for yourWebsite.com.

v. The .com Name Server will have a list of where the local server is for yourWebsite.com. This address will be shared back to the Local Name Server.

vi. The Local Name Server will then query the yourWebsite.com Name Server, which will have the IP address that the laptop was trying to access.

vii. The IP address is sent back to the Local Name Server. The Local Name Server will add this IP address to its records (cache) in case you or anyone else using this Local Name Server ever wants to visit that site again, this record will save time and energy spent finding the IP address.

viii. The Local Name Server will let the Laptop know the IP address.

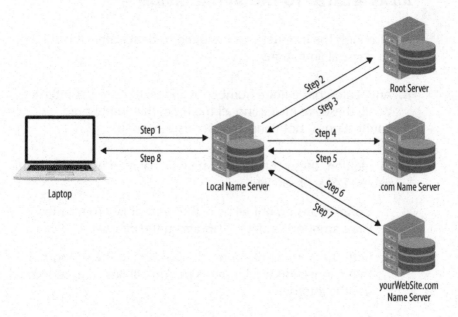

4. This process happens very quickly each time you type a domain name into your browser.

i. It happens automatically for all websites, whether they were added to the internet yesterday or they have been there for twenty years.

    ii.   DNS resolution is one example of many algorithms running on the internet that improve its scalability.

Test Tip

To get a sense of how fast information is traveling back and forth from your computer to locations on the internet, try this tool: ping-test.net. Use the dropdown to ping a location in the list. Notice how in the first test to a location, the variability is quite wide (far away from a horizontal line). Then, ping that same location again and you should notice that this variability decreases. This is partially because the servers are able to resolve the location with fewer requests.

IX. IDEAS RELATED TO THE DIGITAL DIVIDE

A. Although the internet was designed to be scalable, it is subject to physical limitations.

B. Any region has a finite number of connections to the internet. While these are increasing all the time, the number of connections is not consistent across the world.

C. In addition, these connections may be handled using fiber optic cables, DSLs, or satellite.

    1.   Connections do not all have the same ability to transfer large amounts of data to and from the internet.

    2.   Both the number of connections as well as the strength of that connection will impact a person's ability to access and use the internet.

D. People make decisions to connect certain cities and countries faster than others and these choices are not generally related to the number of people in an area.

E. Chapter 18 contains more information about the digital divide.

Check out this site: ourworldindata.org/internet to see how internet access across the world is not equitable. Researching issues that keep our world divided is important to help you see how pivotal access is to our collective movement forward as a world society. This research will also help you practice Data (Chapter 15) and Impact of Computing (Chapter 18), two other key topics in your End-of-Course Exam.

X. IDEAS RELATED TO CIRCUIT SWITCHING VS. PACKET SWITCHING

A. Both circuit switching and packet switching are ways to connect devices.

B. Circuit switching is a connection-oriented form of communication between two points on a network.

1. Circuit switching means a single path will be followed and that two other points in the network cannot use that same path at the same time.

2. Information is received in the same order it was sent.

3. Commonly used for voice communication like older telephone service connections.

4. Look at circuit switching as a Layer 1 (physical) connection.

C. Packet switching is an alternative to circuit switching where packets are divided into smaller units.

1. With packet switching there is no uniform path.

2. Information may be received in a different order from the way it was sent.

3. Commonly used in wireless, some cable modems, DSL and satellite connections.

4. Look at packet switching as a Layer 3 (network) connection.

XI. WHAT YOU NEED TO BE ABLE TO DO WITH COMPUTER SYSTEMS AND NETWORKS

A. Understand bandwidth is a ratio that measures network performance.

1. Bandwidth is the amount of data transported in a certain amount of time.

2. Bandwidth is measured in bits per second.

3. Delays in a network cause bandwidth to decrease.

  i. These delays can be caused by issues within any of the 7 layers in the OSI model.

  ii. Delays can be caused by software, hardware, or both.

B. Consider solutions handled using sequential, parallel, and/or distributed computing.

1. You will need to compare these problem solutions.

2. You will need to determine the efficiency of these solutions.

3. To compare efficiency of solutions, you need to calculate and compare the time it takes each to perform the same task.

  i. A sequential solution takes as long as the sum of all its steps.

  ii. A parallel computing solution takes as long as its sequential tasks plus the longest of its parallel tasks.

4. You will need to calculate the "speedup" of a parallel solution.

  i. The "speedup" is the amount of time it took to complete the task sequentially divided by the time it took to complete the task when done in parallel.

  ii. The greater the "speedup," the more gained from considering a parallel solution.

XII. MULTIPLE-CHOICE QUESTIONS RELATED TO COMPUTER SYSTEMS & NETWORKS

EXAMPLE 1 (SNEAK PEAK):

A certain computer has two identical processors that are able to run in parallel. Each processor can run only one process at a time, and each process must be executed on a single processor. The following table indicates the amount of time it takes to execute each of three processes on a single processor. Assume that none of the processes are dependent on any of the other processes.

Process	Execution Time on Either Processor
X	40 seconds
Y	60 seconds
Z	90 seconds

Which approach should be used to minimize time spent to accomplish all three processes?

- (A) Process X should be run independently. Processes Y and Z should run in parallel.

- (B) Process Y should be run independently. Processes X and Z should run in parallel.

- (C) Process Z should be run independently. Processes X and Y should run in parallel.

- (D) Processes X, Y, and Z should all be run independently.

Answer: (C)

If we processed each task sequentially, the total time spent would be 40 + 60 + 90 = 190 seconds.

A parallel computing solution takes as long as its sequential tasks plus the longest of its parallel tasks.

So, considering each situation separately.

Situation 1 (Y and Z run in parallel):

- See table to the right.

- If Z and Y run in parallel while X runs independently, the longest of the tasks is 150 seconds.

	Process 1	Process 2
	X: 40 sec	Y: 60 sec
		Z: 90 sec
Total Time:	40 sec	*150 sec*

Note that since this is shorter than 190 seconds (the sequential solution), the solution cannot be Choice (D).

Situation 2 (X and Z run in parallel):

- See table at right.

- If X and Y run in parallel while Z runs independently, the longest of the tasks is 130 seconds.

	Process 1	Process 2
	Y: 60 sec	X: 40 sec
		Z: 90 sec
Total Time:	60 sec	*130 sec*

Situation 3 (X and Y run in parallel):

- See table at right.

- If X and Y run in parallel while Z runs independently, the longest of the tasks is 100 seconds.

	Process 1	Process 2
	Z: 90 sec	X: 40 sec
		Y: 60 sec
Total Time:	90 sec	*100 sec*

So the time is minimized when X and Y run in parallel. Situation 3 reflects the minimum possible time, which is 100 seconds.

EXAMPLE 2 (SNEAK PEAK):

Consider Example 1.

Which of the following best approximates the minimum possible time to execute all three processes when the two processors are run in parallel?

(A) 150 seconds

(B) 130 seconds

(C) 100 seconds

(D) 110 seconds

Answer: (C)

See the explanation for Example 1. The least possible time to execute all three processes occurred when X and Y were run in parallel. That should take approximately 100 seconds.

EXAMPLE 3 (SNEAK PEAK):

Consider Example 1.

Which ratio below could be used to estimate the highest possible speedup of the parallel solution?

(A) 190/100

(B) 100/190

(C) 190/150

(D) 130/190

Answer: (A)

If we processed each task sequentially, the total time spent would be 40 + 60 + 90 = 190 seconds. The "speedup" of a parallel solution is calculated by dividing the time it would take to complete the task sequentially by the time it takes to complete the task in parallel. The highest speedup would happen when time is minimized. We know that time is 100 seconds from Example 1. So the highest speedup would be calculated using 190/100.

EXAMPLE 4 (SNEAK PEAK):

Consider Example 1.

Which ratio below could be used to estimate the lowest possible speedup of the parallel solution?

   (A) 19/10

   (B) 15/19

   (C) 19/13

   (D) 19/15

Answer: (D)

Again, speedup is calculated by dividing the time to complete the task sequentially by the time it takes to complete the task in parallel. This time, we are looking for the ratio that would cause the lowest possible speedup. This means we want the parallel solution that required the most time. That was when Y and Z ran in parallel which took approximately 150 seconds. So 190/150 = 19/15.

Test Tip

Examples 1, 2, 3, and 4 each provide a different type of question that you might see on your End-of-Course Exam related to parallel computing, efficiencies, and speedup. It is unlikely that you will see questions for this topic chained together like this on your End-of-Course Exam.

EXAMPLE 5 (SNEAK PEAK):

Which of the following statements is NOT true about parallel and distributed computing?

(A) Distributed computing allows problems to be solved that might not be solvable using a single computer.

(B) When increasing the use of parallel computing in a solution, efficiency is still limited by the sequential part.

(C) Adding parallel portions to a solution does not always lead to increases in efficiency.

(D) Solutions that use sequential computing scale more effectively than solutions that use parallel computing.

Answer: (D)

Choice (A) is a true statement. This is one of the benefits of distributed computing. Choice (B) is true; this is what we used to compare efficiencies in Examples 1–4. Choice (C) is true. Because efficiency is limited by the sequential part of a solution, adding parallel parts would not change the time required to accomplish the sequential part. Choice (D) is not true. Solutions that use *parallel* computing scale more effectively than solutions that use *sequential* computing.

EXAMPLE 6 (SNEAK PEAK):

Read the following statements. Which of these statements is true?

(A) In a fault-tolerant system, there is only one path between sender and receiver.

(B) Routing is the process of finding a path between the sender and receiver.

(C) Redundancy in a system means that the number of components is reduced.

(D) In a fault-tolerant system, if a component fails, the system will shut down.

Answer: (B)

Choice (A) is not a true statement. In a fault-tolerant system, there is more than one path between sender and receiver, in case one of these fails. Choice (B) is correct. This is the definition of routing. Choice (C) is an incorrect statement. The number of components are increased to create redundancy. Choice (D) is incorrect. If a component fails in a fault-tolerant system, other components take over so the system does not fail.

EXAMPLE 7 (SNEAK PEAK):

Suppose your Internet Service Provider claims you will be able to download 100 MB per second. When you tested to see your actual download speed, you saw download speeds of 20 MB per second. What does this mean?

(A) Your observed bandwidth is higher than your Internet Service Provider claimed.

(B) Your observed bandwidth is lower than your Internet Service Provider claimed.

(C) If you used more devices to access the internet, your bandwidth would improve.

(D) If you used an older router, your bandwidth would improve.

Answer: (B)

Choice (B) is correct. Generally observed bandwidth (or actual internet speed) is lower than what ISPs claim. Choices (A), (C), and (D) are all incorrect. Using fewer devices may improve your bandwidth and using a newer router may help as well.

Test Tip

The multiple-choice questions here, in Chapter 19, and online will give you a sense of what you need to know about Computer Systems and Networks, but you can do a lot on your own to review. Many key innovations in our world involve several of these concepts. Read articles about these innovations from sources like NPR Technology Stories (npr.org/sections/technology), Science Daily (sciencedaily.com), or ACM Tech News (technews.acm.org).

Big Idea 5: Impact of Computing

I. OVERVIEW

A. About 21%–26% of the End-of-Course Exam questions will focus on the Impact of Computing.

B. This means you can expect 15–18 questions out of 70 to be focused on this topic.

II. WHAT DOES "IMPACT OF COMPUTING" MEAN?

A. Computer programs impact our society, economy, and culture in intended and unintended ways.

B. It is important that programmers understand:

1. the legal and ethical concerns that come with programs.

2. their responsibility in anticipating these concerns.

C. It is important that all users understand:

1. the risks of sharing personally identifiable information (PII) about themselves.

2. how to take steps to keep themselves safe.

III. QUESTIONS TO ASK YOURSELF

A. What computer program or application do you use every day?

1. Would you have a hard time not using this application? Why?

2. What information did/do you give about yourself to use this application?

B. Are innovators responsible for the harmful effects of their innovations even if these effects were not intended? Why or why not?

C. What data is generated by smartphones and what is this data being used for?

IV. WHAT YOU NEED TO KNOW ABOUT IMPACT OF COMPUTING

A. Key Terms

▸ digital divide: divisions and inequity in our world caused by differing access to computing devices and the internet based on socioeconomic, geographic, or demographic characteristics

▸ bias: prejudice in favor or against a group when compared to another group

▸ crowdsourcing: practice of obtaining input and/or information from a large group of people via the internet

▸ citizen science: scientific research conducted partly or entirely by distributed individuals, many of whom may not be scientists; citizen scientists use their own computing devices to contribute relevant data to research

▸ Creative Commons: public copyright license enabling free distribution of otherwise copyrighted work

▶ open source: copyright license that enables free distribution of programs

▶ open access: copyright license that enables free distribution of research

▶ personally identifiable information (PII): information about an individual that identifies, links, relates, or describes them. Examples include: Social Security number, age, race, address, phone number(s), medical information, financial information, biometric data

▶ authentication: proving you are who you say you are

▶ multifactor authentication: method of computer access control where a user is given access only after presenting at least two pieces of evidence that prove they are who they say they are

▶ authentication mechanism: there are three categories of authentication:

  – knowledge (something a person knows)

  – possession (something a person has)

  – inherence (something a person is)

▶ encryption: process of changing data to prevent unauthorized access

▶ decryption: process of decoding data to see what it was before it was encrypted

▶ symmetric key encryption: common encryption approach that involves one key for both encryption and decryption

▶ public key encryption: common encryption approach that pairs a public key for encryption and a private key for decryption. Sender does not need the receiver's private key to encrypt, but the receiver's private key is required to decrypt the message.

▶ certificate authority: company that issues digital certificates to validate ownership of encryption keys; based on a trust model

> ▸ computer virus: malicious program that can copy itself and gain access to a computer in an unauthorized way; viruses often attach themselves to legitimate programs and then start running independently on a computer

> ▸ malware: software intended to damage or take partial control of a computing system

> ▸ phishing: technique that tries to trick a user into giving away personal information; information can then be used to access online resources like bank accounts.

> ▸ keylogging: use of a program to record user keystrokes to gain access to passwords and other confidential information

> ▸ rogue access point: wireless access point that gives unauthorized access to secure networks; can be used to access, analyze, and manipulate data sent over public networks

 V. WHAT YOU NEED TO UNDERSTAND ABOUT IMPACT OF COMPUTING

A. An effect of a computer program is a change to society, economy, or culture caused by this program being used.

    1. The digital divide is an example of an effect.

        i. Not all people in the world have equal access to computers, technology, and/or the internet.

        ii. This has led to divisions and inequities in our world.

    2. Computing bias is an example of an effect.

        i. If humans or data contains bias, these biases can be written into a program and used by the innovation.

        ii. When this happens, the computing innovation that uses this program inherits this bias.

    3. Crowdsourcing is an example of an effect.

        i. Problems, their solutions, and results are more readily available to more people.

ii. Science and access to scientific data has been improved by "citizen science" projects, where crowdsourcing is applied to solve scientific problems.

4. Legal and ethical concerns are examples of effects.

 i. Computing innovations have led to changes in the amount and type of information that people can access and use.

 ii. As a result, rules governing how people can use this information exist; these should be familiar to all members of our society.

 iii. "Open" materials like those found with Creative Commons, open source, and open access licenses are not all available for you to use as you see fit.

  ▸ These materials come with conditions decided by the author(s).

  ▸ Conditions include:

   – attribution of the material

   – if the material can be used to make money (for financial gain)

   – how to reuse the material

 iv. To use the material legally, you must meet these conditions.

5. Socially and politically we have been impacted by the use of computing innovations.

 i. Not all people have access to technology, leading to a digital divide.

 ii. Algorithms can include bias.

 iii. Some innovations are constantly collecting our data and monitoring our activity.

6. People with bad intentions can use computing programs to their advantage to trick you into accidentally providing too much information, downloading malicious software, or clicking a link.

B. The effect of an innovation is different from the purpose and/or function of an innovation.

1. The effect of an innovation is a change to society, economy, or culture caused by the innovation being used as intended.

2. The purpose of an innovation is about why the innovation was created.

   i. What job is the innovation supposed to be doing?

   ii. The answer to this question is the *purpose*.

3. The function of an innovation is about how the innovation works.

C. It is important that you understand how to protect yourself and others when you are using technology.

1. Follow usage rules when you are using online materials.

2. When using the internet, you should know that a malicious link can be disguised on a web page (including advertisements) or in an email message.

3. Use strong passwords.

   i. A strong password is easy for you to remember but difficult for someone else to guess based on knowledge of that user.

   ii. A strong password should be long enough that it is not vulnerable to an attacker trying many combinations of that password. This is called a brute force attack.

Test Tip

Unsure if your password is strong enough to resist a brute force attack? This site would help you: howsecureismypassword.net. The site will provide an estimate for how long it would take a computer, trying multiple combinations of characters, to break it. In addition, it lists tips to improve the security of your password.

4. Emails can be a source of many attacks.

   i. Be wary of attachments, links, and forms in emails.

   ii. If you do not know the sender, you should not interact with this email.

   iii. If you do know the sender, reach out to the sender by phone or with a separate email to confirm that they sent the email.

   iv. Malicious emails may come from unknown senders or from known senders whose security has been compromised.

5. Untrustworthy (often free) downloads from freeware or shareware sites can contain malware.

6. Data sent over public networks can be intercepted, analyzed, and modified.

7. If you must use a public network:

   i. Do not connect to every public network.

      ▸ The fewer networks you connect to with fewer people, the less likely it is that someone will be attempting to access your data.

      ▸ Be wary of public access forms that require a lot of PII. Consider creating and using an alternative email for these types of forms.

      ▸ Stores that collect this PII will likely use this information to create targeted ads.

   ii. Some browsers will provide a warning when you are connected to a public network and browsing using HTTP rather than encrypted HTTPS. You should notice that warning.

      ▸ When you browse over HTTPS people on the same network as you cannot see the data traveling between you and the server of the website you are accessing.

> ▸ Over HTTP, it is easier for them to see what you are doing.

iii. Close applications that allow you to file share without touching another device are called "frictionless" file share apps. Air Drop is an example.

iv. Read the fine print for what you are signing up for when you join a public network.

> ▸ You do not need to understand every word.

> ▸ Look for "red flags" like: type of data they are collecting, what they are doing with that data

8. To access the internet you might consider:

i. Setting up a hotspot through a smartphone.

ii. Using a virtual private network (VPN).

VI. WHAT YOU NEED TO BE ABLE TO DO WITH IMPACT OF COMPUTING

A. Describe how computing innovations have impacted our society, economy, and culture.

1. Identify intended and unintended effects.

2. Identify beneficial and harmful effects.

B. Explain how people, working together, have impacted the development of solutions. Examples include:

1. crowdsourcing

2. citizen science

C. Consider legal and ethical factors that come from using computing innovations.

1. Understand how to use the amount of information available to you in a legal way.

2. Consider the biases that may be included in a computing innovation and how that could impact you and others if not resolved.

D. Be aware of the risks involved and how to protect yourself from these risks while you are using computing innovations, especially while connected to the internet.

1. Many computing innovations require data to be collected and stored about you.

    i. You should be aware of this and how to protect yourself.

    ii. You will need to be able to describe what could happen as a result of this data being collected.

2. Multifactor authentication—you should be able to see an authentication mechanism and know how this authentication should be classified:

    i. Is it knowledge? (something a person knows)

    ii. Is it possession? (something a person has)

    iii. Is it inherence? (something a person is)

3. Malware

    i. You should know the types of attacks and ways to prevent these attacks.

    ii. You should be able to describe the similarities and differences between types of attacks such as:

    ▸ computer viruses

    ▸ malware

    ▸ phishing

    ▸ keylogging

iii. You should be able to describe the similarities and differences from different sources of these attacks such as:

- ▸ rogue access point
- ▸ downloads
- ▸ emails
- ▸ websites
- ▸ use of public networks

VII. MULTIPLE-CHOICE QUESTIONS RELATED TO THE IMPACT OF COMPUTING

EXAMPLE 1 (SNEAK PEAK):

In an online scam, students in your school were sent an email warning of suspicious activity on the school account. The email asks students to click a link in the email to log into their school account and verify their identity. The email looks legitimate, but clicking the link will open a malicious website with a form that students fill out to verify their identity by providing their name, date of birth, and password. Which of the following best describes the scam?

(A) Phishing

(B) Keylogging

(C) Rogue access point

(D) Multifactor authentication

Answer: (A)

Phishing is an attempt to trick a user into providing personal information. If a student went to the malicious website and provided information to verify their identity, they would be giving personal information away. It is not keylogging. Keylogging is the use of a program to record keystrokes made by a computer user. It is not a rogue access point. A rogue access point is a wireless access point giving people access to a network. It is not multifactor authentication. Authentication is something used to prove you are who you say you are.

EXAMPLE 2 (SNEAK PEAK):

Single sign-on (SSO) is an authentication service that allows a user to use one set of login credentials to login to another 3rd party website.

Which of the following is MOST likely to be a benefit to the user of using SSO instead of creating a new account on the 3rd party website?

(A) The 3rd party website does not need to take the risk of storing the user's password or managing their information.

(B) The user no longer needs a strong password to control access to their account.

(C) The 3rd party website no longer needs to support users if they forget their user name or password.

(D) The user reduces password fatigue because they do not need to remember another user name and password.

Answer: (D)

Choice (D) is correct. Users do benefit because they would not need to remember another user name/ password combination. Choices (A) and (C) are not correct. These are benefits to the 3rd party website. These are reasons a 3rd party website might use SSO instead of creating their own sign-on. Choice (B) is not correct because a user should always put a high priority in choosing a strong password. If it is being used to access more than one account, a strong password controls access to more than one site, making it even more important.

EXAMPLE 3:

Consider the single sign-on approach to authentication in Example 2. Match the form of single sign-on (letters A-C) with the authentication mechanism (Numbers 1–3).

Forms of Single Sign-On	Authentication Mechanism
A. Use your mobile phone to access a 3rd party site.	1. inherence
B. Called "social sign-on," the same user name and password used for a social networking service is used to access a 3rd party site.	2. possession
C. Users scan their fingerprint in their mobile phone and that fingerprint is used to access a 3rd party site.	3. knowledge

Answer: A2, B3, C1

Inherence is something you are. Possession is something you have. Knowledge is something you know. A is about a user having their phone, so A is an example of possession. B is about something the user knows, so B is an example of knowledge. C is about something a user is. The user is human so their fingerprint is unique.

Test Tip

There are no matching questions on the End-of-Course Exam. A multiple-choice question would likely ask about one of these mechanisms. Example 3 is here so you can check your understanding of all three mechanisms.

Examples 4–8 refer to the following article excerpt.

If you resort to deleting apps when your phone's storage space is full, researchers have a solution.

New software "streams" data and code resources to an app from a cloud server when necessary, allowing the app to use only the space it needs on a phone at any given time.

"It's like how Netflix movies aren't actually stored on a computer. They are streamed to you as you are watching them," said Saurabh Bagchi, a Purdue University professor of electrical and computer engineering, and computer science, and director of the Center for Resilient Infrastructures, Systems, and Processes.

"Here the application components, like heavy video or graphics or code paths, are streaming instantly despite the errors and slowdowns that are possible on a cellular network."

Bagchi's team showed in a study how the software, called "AppStreamer," cuts down storage requirements by at least 85% for popular gaming apps on an Android.

The software seamlessly shuffles data between an app and a cloud server without stalling the game. Most study participants didn't notice any differences in their gaming experience while the app used AppStreamer.

Since AppStreamer works for these storage-hungry gaming apps, it could work for other apps that usually take up far less space, Bagchi said. The software also allows the app itself to download faster to a phone.

The researchers will present their findings Feb. 18 at the 17th International Conference on Embedded Wireless Systems and Networks in Lyon, France. Conference organizers have selected this study as one of three top papers.

AppStreamer is a type of software known as middleware, located between the apps on a device and the operating system.

The middleware automatically predicts when to fetch data from a cloud server. AT&T Labs Research provided data from cellular networks for this study to help evaluate which bandwidths AppStreamer would use and how much energy it would consume.

AppStreamer could help phones better accommodate 5G connectivity—high-speed wireless cellular networks that would allow devices to download movies in seconds and handle other data-heavy tasks much faster than the 4G networks currently available to most phones.

> *Using AppStreamer on a 5G network would mean that an app downloads instantly, runs faster and takes up minimal space on a phone.*

Source: Purdue University. "Apps could take up less space on your phone, thanks to new 'streaming' software." ScienceDaily. ScienceDaily, 6 February 2020. <*www.sciencedaily.com/ releases/2020/02/200206184329.htm*>.

Assume the following:

▸ The "Upgraded System" is *AppStreamer*, as described in the article.

▸ The "Original System" is a mobile phone that needs to download applications.

▸ The Original System continues to use and download apps until the phone can no longer perform because it cannot store any more applications.

▸ Then the user needs to decide which applications to delete.

Answer Examples 4–8 are based on the information provided in this reading passage.

EXAMPLE 4 (SNEAK PEAK):

Which of the following is considered a potential effect of *AppStreamer* rather than a function of *AppStreamer*?

(A) *AppStreamer* will allow people to stream applications rather than download applications. This will allow users to have more applications on their phone.

(B) *AppStreamer* will use prediction data to allocate resources you need to use an application. This will allow users to use resources for other activities.

(C) *AppStreamer* will mean that when devices move to 5G, only mobile phone users that have *AppStreamer* will be able to run certain applications. This would increase the digital divide.

(D) *AppStreamer* will mean that more people will be able to have more applications on their phones. This will mean that people will not need to delete applications to save resources.

Answer: (C)

Choice (C) is correct. It is possible that the society of mobile phone users would be divided between those that have *AppStreamer* and those that do not. Those without *AppStreamer* would not be able to have as many applications and would experience greater delays, both of which impact access to technology. This is especially true on a 5G network, based on the article. Choices (A), (B), and (D) are all functions (how *AppStreamer* works) rather than effects.

EXAMPLE 5 (SNEAK PEAK):

Which of the following is the LEAST likely data privacy concern of the updated system?

(A) Your habits such as the type of application you use or the patterns of use will become personal data that is stored about you. This data will be used to predict your age and gender.

(B) Your habits such as the type of application you use or the patterns of use will become personal data that is stored about you. This data will be sold so companies can provide you with targeted advertisements.

(C) You will need to enter a credit card to access certain applications. These applications may store this data in an insecure way and a data breach could occur, compromising your name and credit card information.

(D) Applications contain malware that will be downloaded onto your smartphone. This malware will be used to steal your login credentials for bank software and social media accounts.

Answer: (D)

Choice (D). This computing innovation should reduce if not remove the need to download applications onto your mobile phone. So the concern of malware being downloaded with an application would be least likely. Choices (A), (B), and (C) are all reasonable data concerns.

EXAMPLE 6 (SNEAK PEAK):

Which of the following statements is MOST likely to be true about the tradeoffs of the updated system being used to stream applications?

(A) The updated system will require a strong connection to the internet and, in exchange, you will get less tracking of personal information.

(B) The updated system will provide you with more data privacy, and, in exchange, you will not need as strong of an internet connection for your mobile phone.

(C) The updated system will require a strong connection to the internet and, in exchange, you will not need to use as much room on your mobile phone for applications.

(D) The updated system will provide you with more risk of malware downloads from application stores and, in exchange, you will not need as strong of an internet connection for your mobile phone.

Answer: (C)

Choice (C) is an accurate statement based on the description of the updated system. Choice (A) is incorrect; it is likely there will be more tracking of personal information. Choice (B) is incorrect; it is likely you will have less data privacy and you will need a more robust data connection to support streaming applications. Choice (D) is incorrect because there will be less risk of malware downloads with the updated system.

EXAMPLE 7 (SNEAK PEAK):

Which of the following may be an unintended effect of *AppStreamer*?

I. Games will no longer throttle user experience and will become extremely realistic. People will become addicted to this gaming environment, unable to separate the gaming world from the real world.

II. More people will demand a 5G connection for their devices. 5G connection requires smaller cell phone transmission stations closer to the ground. As a result, taller cell phone towers will not be maintained and people's access to 4G technology will be reduced.

III. More applications will be downloaded than ever before and, as a result, people will be more productive and entertained by using these applications without worrying whether their phone can handle storing them or not.

(A) I, II, and III

(B) II and III only

(C) I and III only

(D) I and II only

Answer: (D)

Choice (D) is correct. The computing innovation was created to help users as described in this statement. This was the intended effect of this computing innovation. I and II introduce two unintended effects of the innovation.

EXAMPLE 8 (SNEAK PEAK):

Of the following potential benefits, which is LEAST likely to be provided by *AppStreamer*?

(A) *AppStreamer* will collect data about users and will use this data to create more targeted advertisements and to find new applications that meet the demand of their users.

(B) *AppStreamer* will not collect user data about personal preferences while they are using applications. This way, users' personal information will remain more secure.

(C) *AppStreamer* will provide better information to users about what they can expect from each application so that users can find what they are looking for in a more efficient way.

(D) *AppStreamer* will cause applications to be more realistic since they would no longer be limited by the storage capacity of users' mobile phones.

Answer: (B)

Choice (B) is correct. It is very likely that *AppStreamer* would work like other comparable online streaming apps and collect user data about preferences. These preferences would likely be sold to companies looking to create targeted advertisements. Choices (A), (C), and (D) are all likely effects of this computing innovation.

Test Tip

Examples 4–8 were created to give you an idea of what Reading Passage Multiple-Choice Questions will look like on the End-of-Course Exam. To prepare for these types of questions, research and learn about new computing innovations. Write and reflect about the function, purpose, beneficial effects, harmful effects, and data privacy concerns, data storage concerns, and data security concerns of the computing innovation.

EXAMPLE 9 (SNEAK PEAK):

Which of the following statements explain how bias can exist in a computing innovation.

    I.   Algorithms can contain the same biases of the people that write them.

    II. If biased data is used in training sets for artificial intelligence, then resulting algorithms will include the bias.

    III. Bias can be embedded at all levels of software development.

(A) I and II only

(B) II and III only

(C) I and III only

(D) I, II, and III

Answer: (D)

Choice (D) is correct. All three statements are examples of how bias can exist in a computing innovation.

EXAMPLE 10 (SNEAK PEAK):

Which of the following is NOT a legal way to use material created by someone else?

(A) Download program code that someone else created and stored on an open source website. Build a larger program that uses their code and cite their code in your final product.

(B) Use a research article you found on an open access website to learn about a computing innovation. Create a slide show that shows your learning and cite the article using an MLA citation tool.

(C) Use a public domain image you found on a Creative Commons site. Since it is listed as public domain, no citation is necessary.

(D) Use an image you found on a Creative Commons site on a product that you intend to sell for profit. Attribute the author as specified on the site. The attribution statement does not have an "NC" (non-commercial) marking in it.

Answer: (C)

Choice (C) is correct because citations are always necessary for media that you did not create. The appropriate citation for a public domain image is to write, "public domain." Choices (A), (B), and (D) are examples of legal use. Choice (D) is legal because media that should not be used for commercial gain must be listed as "NC" (non-commercial). Without NC in the attribution statement, the author is giving permission for you to use the image for commercial gain with a citation.

Test Tip

Computing innovations have a profound impact on the world around us. While these few examples give you a sense of what to expect on the End-of-Course Exam, this should be the beginning of your study of the Impact of Computing. Continue reading articles about these innovations from sources like NPR Technology Stories (npr.org/sections/technology), Science Daily (sciencedaily.com), or ACM Tech News (technews.acm.org).

Practice Multiple-Choice Questions

Each of the AP®-style practice questions below is followed by four answer choices. Select the one that is best in each case. (In some cases, where indicated, you must select two answers.) Remember to use the Exam Reference Sheet for information about the pseudocode used on the exam. The reference is located in Appendix E of your *Crash Course*. Answers and explanations directly follow this section. For a full-length practice exam, go online at *www.rea.com/studycenter*.

1. A person wants to move an image from one device to a second device. Which of the following scenarios best demonstrates the use of lossy compression of the original file?

   (A) An algorithm is run on the image so that repeated pixel colors are stored in a more efficient way. This algorithm causes the image to reduce in size and changes the file type. On the second device, the image can be viewed easily using the new file type.

   (B) An application compresses the image before it is sent. On the second device, the same application restores the compressed file to its original version before the image is viewable.

   (C) The image is transmitted from the first device to the second device. The second device views the image.

   (D) An algorithm is run on the image so that similar pixel colors are stored as the same color. This algorithm causes the image to reduce in size and changes the file type. On the second device, the image can be viewed easily using the new file type.

2. In a certain camp, a child must be at least 7 years old to participate in horseback riding and at least 9 years old to use the zipline. A child must be younger than 19 years of age to participate in camp. The variable age represents the age of the child as an integer.

   Which of the following expressions evaluates to `true` if the child is old enough to participate in zipline and young enough to participate in camp?

   I. `(age > 9) AND (age ≤ 18)`

   II. `(age ≥ 9) AND (age ≤ 18)`

   III. `NOT(age < 9) AND (age < 19)`

   (A) I only

   (B) II only

   (C) II and III only

   (D) I and III only

3. The following procedure is intended to return the number of times the value goal is exceeded in the list sales. The procedure does not work as intended.

```
Line 1:  PROCEDURE countNumTimesSalesGoalExceeded(sales, goal)
Line 2:  {
Line 3:     count ← 0
Line 4:     FOR EACH item IN sales
Line 5:     {
Line 6:        IF (item > goal)
Line 7:        {
Line 8:           count ← count + 1
Line 9:        }
Line 10:       RETURN(count)
Line 11:    }
Line 12: }
```

Which of the following changes can be made so that the procedure will work as intended?

(A) Changing line 6 to IF(item ≥ goal)

(B) Changing line 6 to IF(sales[item] > goal)

(C) Moving the statement in line 3 so it appears between lines 5 and 6

(D) Moving the statement in line 10 so it appears between lines 11 and 12

4. Suppose a sorted list contains 1000 elements. How many iterations would be required to use binary search to determine if a value is in this list?

(A) 1000

(B) 100

(C) 10

(D) 1

5. A certain computer has two identical processors that are able to run in parallel. Each processor can run only one process at a time, and each process must be executed on a single processor. The following table indicates the amount of time it takes to execute each of three processes on a single processor. Assume that none of the processes are dependent on any of the other processes.

Process	Execution Time on Either Processor
X	40 seconds
Y	60 seconds
Z	50 seconds

Assume that the speedup calculation is based on the minimum possible time to execute all three processes when two processors are run in parallel. Which of the following best approximates the speedup of this parallel solution?

(A) $\dfrac{150}{100}$

(B) $\dfrac{150}{90}$

(C) $\dfrac{150}{50}$

(D) $\dfrac{150}{40}$

6. Order the following list of binary numbers from least to greatest: 1101, 0101, 1110, 0111

(A) 0101, 0111, 1101, 1110

(B) 0111, 0101, 1101, 1110

(C) 0101, 0111, 1110, 1101

(D) 0101, 1110, 1101, 0111

7. In the following statement, b1, b2, and sol are Boolean variables.

sol ← NOT b1 OR b2

Which of the following code segments produce the same result as the statement above for all possible values of b1 and b2?

(A)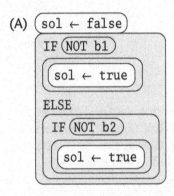

(B)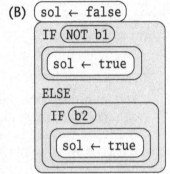

(C)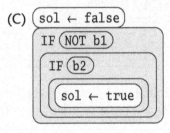

(D)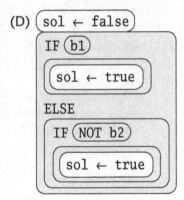

8. Consider the following procedures:

Procedure Call	Explanation
getPartOfString theString, index1, index2	Returns a substring of theString. The substring is from index1 to index2, not including index2. So, getPartOfString("ABCD", 1,3) would return "AB".
find theString, letter	Returns the location of a letter in a string. So, find("ABCD","B") would return 2.

The following code segment is intended to set domainExtension equal to the domain extension of the string variable websiteAddress. The code segment does not work as intended in all cases.

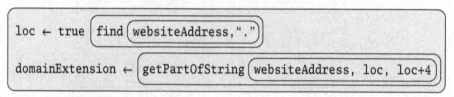

```
loc ← true find(websiteAddress,".")

domainExtension ← getPartOfString(websiteAddress, loc, loc+4)
```

Which of the following initial value for websiteAddress can be used to show that the code segment does not work as intended?

(A) "ABCD.com"

(B) "ABC.edu"

(C) "AB.biz"

(D) "ABC.co"

9. The following grid contains a robot represented as a triangle. The robot is initially facing left.

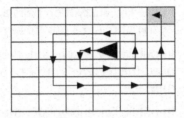

Which of the following code segments can be used to move the robot to the gray square along the path indicated by the arrows?

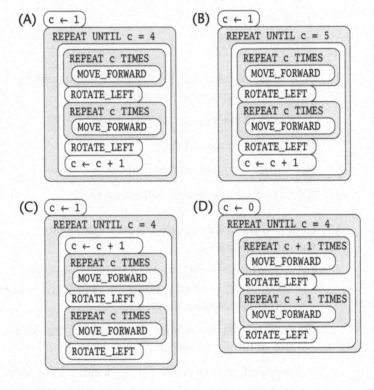

(A)
```
c ← 1
REPEAT UNTIL c = 4
    REPEAT c TIMES
        MOVE_FORWARD
    ROTATE_LEFT
    REPEAT c TIMES
        MOVE_FORWARD
    ROTATE_LEFT
    c ← c + 1
```

(B)
```
c ← 1
REPEAT UNTIL c = 5
    REPEAT c TIMES
        MOVE_FORWARD
    ROTATE_LEFT
    REPEAT c TIMES
        MOVE_FORWARD
    ROTATE_LEFT
    c ← c + 1
```

(C)
```
c ← 1
REPEAT UNTIL c = 4
    c ← c + 1
    REPEAT c TIMES
        MOVE_FORWARD
    ROTATE_LEFT
    REPEAT c TIMES
        MOVE_FORWARD
    ROTATE_LEFT
```

(D)
```
c ← 0
REPEAT UNTIL c = 4
    REPEAT c + 1 TIMES
        MOVE_FORWARD
    ROTATE_LEFT
    REPEAT c + 1 TIMES
        MOVE_FORWARD
    ROTATE_LEFT
```

10. Which of the following statements about public key encryption is true?

    I.   Public key encryption pairs a public key for encryption and a private key for decryption.

    II. In public key encryption, the sender does not need the receiver's private key to encrypt a message.

    III. In public key encryption, the receiver's private key is required to decrypt the message.

(A) I only

(B) I and III only

(C) II and III only

(D) I, II, and III

11. Which of the following information do packets need to be routed from source to destination?

(A) Code so packet can be processed

(B) Planned route of travel

(C) Source and destination addresses

(D) List of addresses reached en route

12. Which of the following policies is most likely to worsen the digital divide?

(A) A school allows students to bring laptops into school to complete assignments faster than school computers would allow.

(B) All students in a school are given a laptop for their use at home and school.

(C) A city offers free classes on a monthly basis to help anyone learn how to access and use the internet.

(D) A community organization raises money to install free mobile access locations in areas that have not had internet access.

13. A list of numbers has n elements, indexed from 1 to n. The following algorithm is intended to display the location of the smallest number in the list. The algorithm uses the variables smallestNum and pos. Steps 3 and 4 are missing.

Step 1: Set smallestNum to the value stored in the first index.
Step 2: Set pos to 1.
Step 3: (missing step)
Step 4: (missing step)
Step 5: Repeat steps 3 and 4 until the value of pos is greater than n.
Step 6: Display the value of smallestNum.

Which of the following could be used to replace steps 3 and 4 so that the algorithm works as intended?

(A) Step 3: If the value stored in the list at position pos is less than smallestNum, set smallestNum to the value stored in the list at position pos.
Step 4: Increase the value of pos by 1.

(B) Step 3: Increase the value of pos by 1.
Step 4: If the value stored in the list at position pos is less than smallestNum, set smallestNum to the value stored in the list at position pos.

(C) Step 3: If the value stored in the list at position pos is greater than smallestNum, set smallestNum to the value stored in the list at position pos.
Step 4: Increase the value of pos by 1.

(D) Step 3: Increase the value of pos by 1.
Step 4: If the value stored in the list at position pos is greater than smallestNum, set smallestNum to the value stored in the list at position pos.

14. Consider the following program, which uses the variables x, y, and z.

```
x ← 0
y ← 10
z ← 5
y ← z
x ← x + y
DISPLAY (x)
DISPLAY (y)
```

What is displayed when this program runs?

(A) 5 5

(B) 5 15

(C) 5 0

(D) 15 5

15. Consider the two programs below.

Program A:

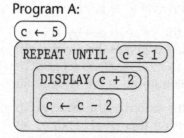

Program B:

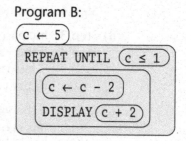

Which of the following best compares the values displayed by programs A and B?

(A) Program A and Program B display identical values.

(B) Program A and Program B display the same values in different orders.

(C) Program A and Program B display the same number of values, but the values differ.

(D) Program A and Program B display a different number of values.

16. Which number is largest?

(A) Binary 1010

(B) Decimal 11

(C) Binary 1100

(D) Decimal 10

17. Which of the following is a consequence of using bits to represent data?

    I.   Storing integers as bits means that some operations may not work correctly on integer values.

    II.   Languages have limits on the size of integers that can be represented using bits.

    III. The fixed number of bits used to represent real numbers causes some numbers to be represented as approximations.

(A) I and II

(B) I and III

(C) II and III

(D) I, II, and III

| Questions 18–22 refer to |
| the information below. |

- A small team of researchers is conducting a study on rainfall amounts at study sites to help farmers make better decisions in planting crops. The researchers broaden the study to include more locations by using a "citizen science" approach to collecting data. Researchers did this to involve more people in climate studies and to get access to more data than they can currently gather on only their sites.

- The team updated their data collection application and approach when they included more locations. Researchers interacted with the original application using a site number to identify the site where rainfall data was collected and an analog tool to collect the data. Researchers interact with the updated application using GPS coordinates to identify the location where rainfall data is being collected and a digital tool to be used with the application.

- Both applications store all information from all sites in a database for future reference. This includes site location information and rainfall data (name of the scientist doing data collection, number of inches of water on the ground, temperature, etc.). The stored data types and categories will be the same for both applications.

- The original application and the updated application are described in the following flowcharts. Each flowchart uses the following blocks.

Block	Explanation
Oval	The start of the algorithm
Parallelogram	An input or output step
Diamond	A conditional or decision step, where execution proceeds to the side labeled "Yes" if the answer to the question is yes and the side labeled "No" if the answer to the question is no
Rectangle	The result of the algorithm

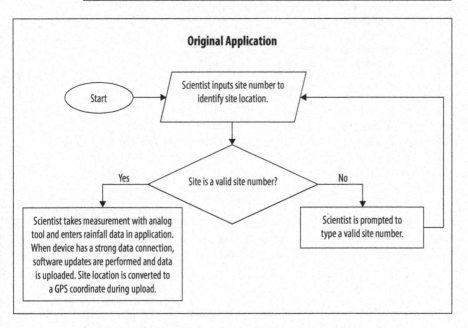

Original Application

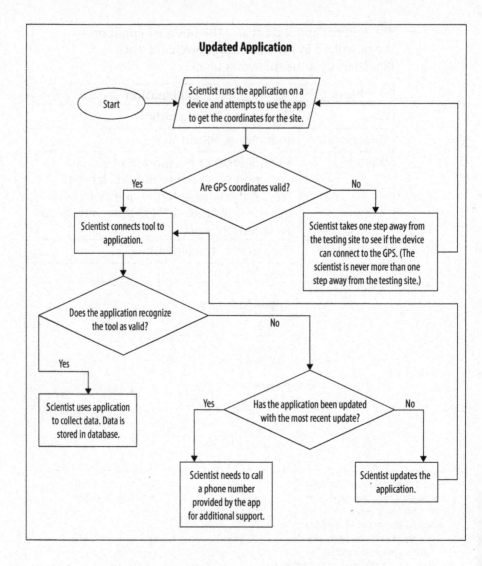

18. Which of the following input data is needed by the updated application that was NOT needed by the original system?

   (A) The phone number for the scientist that is trying to collect data

   (B) The GPS coordinates of the site

(C) The rainfall data such as number of inches of rain, etc.

(D) The files related to performing application updates

19. Which of the following data is necessary for the rainfall application to process in order to enable results to be useful to predict rainfall in a location?

(A) The GPS location needs to be valid and recognized by the application.

(B) The rainfall amount needs to be more than what was predicted.

(C) The rainfall amount needs to be less than what was predicted.

(D) The citizen scientist needs to be part of the original team of researchers.

20. Which of the following is considered a potential effect of the application rather than a purpose of the application?

(A) Scientists are not able to perform data collection because the GPS fails to connect.

(B) Because more data will be collected, the database size will increase at a rate that is too high for the software to be able to handle.

(C) Farmers around the world will be able to predict where and when crops should be planted to increase yield.

(D) More people will be able to contribute to studying the rainfall amounts in different parts of the world.

21. Which of the following may be an unintended effect of the use of the updated application?

    (A) Data accuracy decreases due to errors caused by the measurement tool or GPS readings by people working as citizen scientists.

    (B) Insurance companies use the rainfall data as flood prediction data to increase insurance rates for people in an area where high rainfall is likely to happen.

    (C) Only certain countries can use this application due to the cost of the application and the need to train citizen scientists.

    (D) The increase in the amount of data leads to more accurate estimates of rainfall amounts throughout the world.

22. Which of the following groups is LEAST likely to benefit from the better predictions of rainfall amounts for a given location, assuming they all have access to the predictions?

    (A) Farmers planning to plant crops

    (B) Insurance company executives

    (C) People planning to buy land

    (D) Landowners

Directions: For each of the questions or incomplete statements below, two of the suggested answers are correct. For each of these questions, you must select both correct choices to earn credit. No partial credit will be earned if only one correct choice is selected.

23. Consider the following procedure.

Procedure Call	Explanation
drawShape(xPos, yPos, len)	Draw two line segments of length `len` with common endpoint (xPos, yPos) in common. The second endpoint for the first segment is (xPos-len, yPos). The second endpoint for the second segment is (xPos, yPos+len).

The drawShape procedure is to be used to draw the following figure on a coordinate grid.

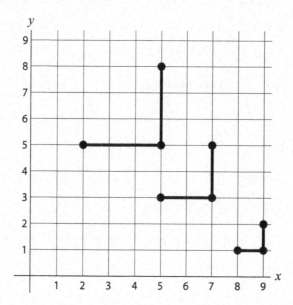

Which of the following code segments could be used to draw this pattern? **Select <u>two</u> answers.**

```
(A) a ← 9
    i ← 0
    REPEAT 3 TIMES
    {
       drawSquare(a - (2 * i),2 * i + 1,i + 1)
       i ← i + 1
    }

(B) a ← 9
    b ← 1
    c ← 1
    REPEAT 3 TIMES
    {
       a ← a - 2
       b ← b + 2
       c ← c + 1
       drawSquare(a, b, c)
    }

(C) a ← 9
    b ← 1
    c ← 1
    REPEAT 3 TIMES
    {
       drawSquare(a, b, c)
       a ← a - 2
       b ← b + 2
       c ← c + 1
    }

(D) a ← 9
    i ← 1
    REPEAT 3 TIMES
    {
       drawSquare(a - (2 * i),2 * i + 1,i + 1)
       i ← i + 1
    }
```

24. A company uses strategies to prevent unauthorized individuals from accessing information that is private to the company. The newest security measure they have added is that all emails with links will be checked by a new software application. The application will compare the link(s) to known malicious links and the email will only be delivered if it does not contain a link that is known to be malicious. Which of the following would be reduced as a result of this new security measure? **Select two answers.**

(A) Keylogging

(B) Rogue access points

(C) Phishing attacks

(D) Multifactor authentication

25. A flowchart is a way to visually represent an algorithm. The flowchart below is used by a movie rating website to set the variable `recommended` to `true` for movies that meet certain criteria.

Block	Explanation
Oval ⬭	The start or end of the algorithm.
Diamond ◇	A conditional or decision step, where execution proceeds to the side labeled true if the condition is true and to the side labeled false otherwise.
Rectangle ▭	One or more processing steps, such as a statement that assigns a value to a variable.

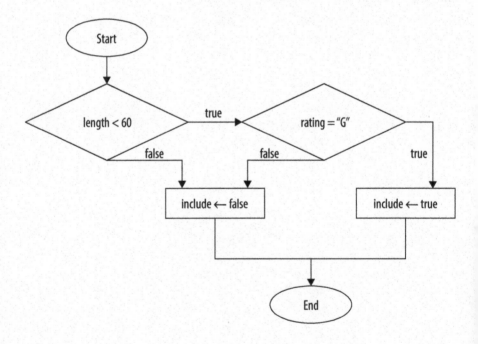

Which of the following statements is equivalent to the algorithm in the flowchart? **Select two answers.**

(A) include ← (length < 60) AND (rating = "G")

(B) include ← NOT((length ≥ 60) OR (rating ≠ "G"))

(C) include ← (length < 60) OR (rating = "G")

(D) include ← NOT((length ≥ 60) AND (rating ≠ "G"))

SOLUTIONS:

1. Correct solution: (D) Lossy compression means that some data is lost and cannot be retrieved. Storing pixels that are similar in color as the same color means that those small color changes cannot be retrieved again.

2. Correct solution: (C) The age variable would need to be in this set {9, 10, 11, . . ., 17, 18}. I is not correct because age > 9 would not include 9. II correctly includes 9, 18, and all integers between. III is correct because NOT(age < 9) is equivalent to age ≥ 9 and age < 19 is equivalent to age ≤ 18.

3. Correct solution: (D) Returning the count variable in the loop will mean that count will be at most 1. The return statement will redirect control from the loop to handle the return. The count value should be returned after all of the items in the sales list have been viewed. By moving line 10 so it appears between lines 11 and 12, this will mean that the loop will correctly traverse the list before returning the count variable.

4. Correct solution: (C) $\log_2(1000)$ is approximately 10.

5. Correct solution: (B) A parallel computing solution takes as long as its sequential tasks plus the longest of its parallel tasks.

Consider each situation separately.

There are no sequential tasks to worry about, only parallel tasks. We need to compare each of the three possible situations separately.

Situation 1 (Y and Z run in parallel):

	Process 1	Process 2
	X: 40 sec	Z: 50 sec
		Y: 60 sec
Total Time:	40 sec	110 sec

So, if Z and Y run in parallel while X runs independently, the longest of the tasks is 110 seconds.

Situation 2 (X and Y run in parallel):

	Process 1	Process 2
	Z: 50 sec	X: 40 sec
		Y: 60 sec
Total Time:	50 sec	100 sec

So, if X and Y run in parallel while Z runs independently, the longest of the tasks is 100 seconds.

Situation 3 (X and Z run in parallel):

	Process 1	Process 2
	Y: 60 sec	X: 40 sec
		Z: 50 sec
Total Time:	60 sec	90 sec

So, if X and Z run in parallel while Y runs independently, the longest of the tasks is 90 seconds.

So the time is minimized when X and Z run in parallel. Situation 3 reflects the minimum possible time, which is 90 seconds.

The speedup is calculated by dividing the time to complete a task sequentially by the time to complete the task in parallel. We know from above that the time to complete the task in parallel is 90 seconds. The time to complete the task sequentially would be $40 + 60 + 50 = 150$ seconds. So the speedup would be $\dfrac{150}{90}$.

6. Correct solution: (A) In any number system, the most significant digit is the leftmost digit. Lining up the numbers vertically, the two numbers 1101 and 1110 are the only numbers with a 1 in the leftmost position, so these are the two largest. Looking at these next to each other 1101 has a zero in the 2's place while 1110 has a 1 in the 2's place, so 1110 is larger than 1101.

   1101

   1110

   Looking at the numbers 0101 and 0111 in the same manner, 0111 has to be larger than 0101. So the correct order is, as written in (A): 0101, 0111, 1101, 1110.

7. Correct solution: (B). (A) OR (B) is logically equivalent to IF/ELSE since (A) OR (B) is true if either (A) is true or (B) is true.

8. Correct solution: (D) The domain extension is located to the right of the period. While many common extensions are 3 letters (.com, .edu, etc.), there are many two letter extensions. A two-letter extension would be a problem with this algorithm because the call to getPartOfString will return the piece of websiteAddress from loc to loc+4. This would work for a 3-letter domain extension, as shown in (A), (B), and (C), but not a 2-letter extension as shown in (D).

9. Correct solution: (B) Notice what happens as the robot moves around the grid. The following table will organize the robots motion by the motion from when the robot is point left (to start) to when the robot returns to point in the same direction, calling this a "circle":

Innermost circle (first "circle")	Second "circle" (after the first circle is done)	Third "circle" (after the second circle is done)	Fourth "circle" (after the third circle is done)
MOVE_FORWARD ROTATE_LEFT MOVE_FORWARD ROTATE_LEFT	MOVE_FORWARD MOVE_FORWARD ROTATE_LEFT MOVE_FORWARD MOVE_FORWARD ROTATE_LEFT	MOVE_FORWARD MOVE_FORWARD MOVE_FORWARD ROTATE_LEFT MOVE_FORWARD MOVE_FORWARD MOVE_FORWARD ROTATE_LEFT	MOVE_FORWARD MOVE_FORWARD MOVE_FORWARD MOVE_FORWARD ROTATE_LEFT MOVE_FORWARD MOVE_FORWARD MOVE_FORWARD MOVE_FORWARD ROTATE_LEFT

Notice that for each "circle" the number of MOVE_FORWARD operations is equal to the "circle" number. The only solution that correctly implements the algorithm is (B).

Let's trace (B):

Value of c at start of the "REPEAT UNTIL c=5" iteration	How many MOVE_FORWARD commands will occur in this iteration?	Value of c at the end of the "REPEAT UNTIL c=5" iteration (note: this will be the value checked against the condition c=5)
1	1	2
2	2	3
3	3	4
4	4	5 (which breaks the loop!)

So the solution cannot be (A) since the loop would break before the final outer "circle" was created. The solution cannot be (C) since the value of c at the start of the loop would be too high. The first "circle" should be created by 1 MOVE_FORWARD command. Incrementing c by 1 at the start of the loop would mean that MOVE_FORWARD would happen twice in that first iteration. (D) is not the solution because the c variable would never be increased. It would remain c + 1 = 1 for all iterations of the "REPEAT UNTIL c=5" loop.

10. Correct solution: (D) By definition, these three statements are true about public key encryption.

11. Correct solution: (C) The packet contains the IP addresses of the sending and receiving host. It is not (A) because the code/software would be located within stops along the network, not within the packet itself. It is not (B) because packets can be assembled in order, out of order, or not at all. The packet does not know or store its planned route of travel. This largely depends on what happens as the packet moves from source to destination. It is not (D). The packet does not gain data while it moves through the data stream. It would not maintain a list of addresses.

12. Correct solution: (A) Not every student would have the ability to bring in a laptop so access to this technology would not be equitable. The other three options are examples of things that may help to decrease the digital divide.

13. Correct solution: (B) Since smallestNum is already set to the value in the first position, Step 3 should increase pos by 1 to look at the value in the second position. Then, to decide if something is a minimum, each step should compare the current smallestNum with the value stored at each element of the list. If the value in the list is less than smallestNum, the algorithm would have found a new minimum. The only option that first increments pos by 1 and then correctly describes this algorithm is (B).

(A) is not correct because the algorithm described in (A) would not fully traverse the list. The last element in the list would not be considered. (D) is not correct because the algorithm described would find the maximum rather than the minimum. (C) has the incorrect algorithm listed. In addition, (C) would not fully traverse the list.

14. Correct solution: (A) To begin, x is 0, y is 10, and z is 5. After line 4 (y ← z), y is assigned 5. Then after line 5 (x ← x + y), x is assigned 0 + 5 or 5. So both x and y are 5.

15. Correct solution: (C) Program A starts with c as 5. The first line of code in the loop is to display 5+2 which is 7. Then c is assigned 3. At the top of the loop, 3+2 is displayed. So 5 is displayed. At the bottom of the last loop iteration, c is assigned 1, breaking the loop. So, in total the code in Program A would display two values: 7 then 5. In Program B, c is assigned c - 2 before the DISPLAY is called. The first value that would be displayed is 5. Then in the next loop, c is assigned 1, so 3 is displayed. In total, Program B would display two values: 5 then 3. The answer is (C) because both programs display two values, but their values differ.

16. Correct solution: (C) Binary 1010 is equivalent to 8 + 2 = 10, in decimal. Binary 1100 is equivalent to 8 + 4 = 12 in decimal. 12 is larger than all other values.

17. Correct solution: (D) I, II, and III are all consequences of using bits to represent data. Each may lead to specific errors, as well. I may lead to overflow errors. II is associated with memory limitations. III may be classified as round-off errors.

18. Correct solution: (B) The solution is not (A) because, although the scientist may need to call if there is an issue, the scientist does not need to provide a phone number to use the app. It is not (C) because the rainfall data has not changed from the original application to

the second application; only the device used to input the data changed. It is not (D) because a software update is not equivalent to the rainfall data being stored by the application. The update may be needed for the rainfall data to be stored correctly. It is (B) because the GPS coordinates were stored based on the site number by the original app. Because sites could be located anywhere in the world, GPS coordinates are necessary inputs at the time of data collection.

19. Correct solution: (A) The solution is not (B) or (C) because predictions should be based on actual data, not assumptions about the data. The solution is not (D) because if the tools work as specified the person collecting the data should not matter; the GPS coordinates and the digital measurement tool should provide reliable results. The GPS data (A) is important because the rainfall amount would be connected to that location.

20. Correct solution: (C) Note that the purposes of the application were identified in this sentence: "Researchers did this to involve more people in climate studies and to get access to more data than they can currently gather on only their sites." The solution is not (A) because the GPS failing to connect is caused by the innovation not working as intended. It is not an effect of the rainfall collection app. It is not (B) because this was caused by the way the data was stored, not the application itself. It is not (D) because this was one of the identified purposes of the application. It is (C) because this is an effect on our world that is caused by the innovation being used as intended.

21. Correct solution: (B) The solution is not (A) because errors caused by the tool or the people working as citizen scientists are not the fault of the application being used as intended. The solution is not (C) because the cost of the application is not an effect of the application. The solution is not (D) because the because

this was an intended effect. The solution is (B) because the study was not intended for insurance companies to use to price insurance.

22. Correct solution: (D) The solution is (D) because landowners already own the land. Whether high amounts of rainfall are predicted or not, it is likely they will need to invest some amount of money to address the issue. Examples are: sell the property, create a way to redirect water, and/or pay for insurance. The solution is not (A) because the farmer could adjust the crop type or perhaps not plant in that section of their land. It is not (B) because it is likely that insurance companies will benefit. These increased predictions will allow them to better price insurance which will lead to increased profit. It is not (C) because people who plan to purchase land can make better choices using these predictions.

23. Correct solutions: (A), (C). The best way to see these solutions is to do a bit of tracing.

Let's trace (A) to see why it works.

Iteration Number	Before call to drawSquare, a =	Before call to drawSquare, i =	Call to drawSquare
1	9	0	Substituting values for i and a, drawSquare(9-(2*0), 2*0+1, 0+1) = drawSquare(9,1,1). This would successfully draw the pattern in the bottom right of the plane.
2	9	1	Substituting values for i and a, drawSquare(9-(2*1), 2*1+1, 1+1) = drawSquare(7,3,2). This would successfully draw the pattern in the center of the plane.
3	9	2	Substituting values for i and a, drawSquare(9-(2*2), 2*2+1, 2+1) = drawSquare(5,5,3). This would successfully draw the pattern in the top left of the plane.

Let's trace (C) to see why it works.

Iteration Number	Before calling drawSquare, a =	Before calling drawSquare, b =	Before calling drawSquare, c =	Call to drawSquare
1	9	1	1	drawSquare(9,1,1). This would successfully draw the pattern in the bottom right of the plane.
2	7	3	2	drawSquare(7,3,2). This would successfully draw the pattern in the center of the plane.
3	5	5	3	drawSquare(5,5,3). This would successfully draw the pattern in the top left of the plane.

So, if (A) and (C) work, look again at (B) and (D). In (B), the problem is that in the loop the changes to a, b, and c happen before the call to drawSquare rather than after. For the values a, b, and c are initialized with, this sequence would not call drawSquare with the correct values. With (D), i is initialized to 1. This would cause the first call to drawSquare to be with parameters (7, 3, 2). Although 2 out of the 3 figures would be correct, the loop would never iterate to create the bottom right shape.

24. Correct solutions: (B), (C). Rogue access points can be created via links in an email. Clicking the link would provide a wireless access point to the network without informing the user. Phishing attacks try to trick people into giving up personal information. One of the ways these attacks are carried out are by embedding links inside emails that try to convince you to click the link. The link would then collect this information. This security measure would prevent these two types of attack. The solution is not (A) since keylogging is the use of a program to record keystrokes in the hopes that some

confidential information like a password is recorded. This would not typically be executed via a link in an email. The solution is not (D) since multifactor authentication is a security measure, not a type of attack.

25. Correct solutions: (A), (B). In order for include to be assigned true, both length<60 <u>and</u> rating = "G" must be true. That is equivalent to (A). Using DeMorgan's Laws, we can look at (B) and see that (B) is logically equivalent to (A):

NOT((length ≥ 60) OR (rating ≠ "G")) is equivalent to:

    NOT(length ≥ 60) AND NOT(rating ≠ "G").

NOT (length ≥ 60) is the same as (length < 60).

Similarly, NOT (rating ≠ "G") is equivalent to (rating = "G").

So NOT((length ≥ 60) OR (rating ≠ "G")) is equivalent to:

    (length < 60) AND (rating = "G").

The solution cannot be (C) since the logical operation is OR rather than AND. The solution cannot be (D) since (D) is equivalent to (C), using DeMorgan's Laws.

Strategies for Success on the End-of-Course Exam

Your AP® CS Principles End-of-Course Exam will consist of 70 multiple-choice questions administered in one two-hour testing session. These questions will be about Creative Development, Data, Algorithms and Programming, Computer Systems and Networks, and Impact of Computing. About 74%–79% of this exam is about the first four topics. The Impact of Computing topic makes up the remaining 21%–26% of the exam.

The score you achieve on the multiple-choice section of the exam will be based on the number of questions answered correctly. Each question has four options (A–D). The majority of the questions have one correct answer. About 8 of the 70 questions have two correct answers. These are grouped together at the end of the exam. There is no partial credit and there are no penalties for incorrect answers or unanswered questions.

You should have plenty of time to understand and answer each question, or at least make an educated guess.

Here are some test-taking tips to keep in mind:

1. **Answer all related questions together.** One prompt may have more than one question related to that prompt. *Do not skip over these related questions.* Once you invest the time reading the prompt, skipping questions will mean you have to reread the prompt later, which will take away time from answering other questions.

2. **Use the process of elimination.** Success is as much about finding the correct answer as it is about getting rid of the wrong answers! Use your subject knowledge

to cross out as many of the wrong answer choices as possible.

3. **Be ready to apply your skills and understanding.** The multiple-choice questions are not about vocabulary or recalling specific details of how a part of a computer or a computing innovation works. The questions are about applying what you know about these details to show your understanding and that you have practiced the necessary skills.

4. **Watch your time.** If you are spending more than 2–3 minutes on a question, make an educated guess and move on. If you finish your exam and you have time left, review your responses. If there are questions you have not answered, make your best guess.

5. **Answer all questions.** Points are not deducted for wrong answers. It is in your best interest to answer all of the questions.

6. **Circle key command words in a question.** Circle words like EXCEPT, ALL, NOT, or BEST. If you're reading the question quickly, you might miss seeing these all-important commands. Be sure to focus on the logic of the question.

7. **Pay attention to your bubble sheet.** Make sure that you have entered your answers correctly on the bubble sheet. If you are working on question 4, be sure you fill in the bubble for question 4. If you lose your place and put the answer for question 4 in the bubble for question 5, it will throw off your entire answer sheet and your score.

8. **Think of your answer first.** Read the question and think of your answer first, before you read the answer choices given. This can help you select the best choice rather than falling into distracting traps presented by the wrong answer choice.

PART III
APPENDICES

Glossary of AP® Computer Science Principles Terms

abstract data types (ADT's)—lists and other collections used to develop programs

abstraction—reducing complexity in a program to help improve focus on a relevant concept or to understand or solve a problem; often involves hiding irrelevant details

acknowledgment of code—credit given to another creator who built code that you used; often handled in coding comments

algorithm—a finite group of instructions that work together to accomplish a larger task; consist of sequence, selection, and/or iteration

ALU (Arithmetic Logic Unit)—performs arithmetic and logical operations on numbers stored in registers of CPU

analog data—data with values that is continuous or smooth; examples: volume of music, dimmer switch

analog to digital converter—device that converts analog data to digital data; example: sound card

anonymity software—software that hides your browsing history and prevents use of cookies to track your data

anti-exploit software—security software that identifies malware that might be missed by traditional antivirus software; uses behavioral clues

antivirus software—program that scans files as they arrive, leave, or are executed in order to prevent a virus from harming your computer

append (in list operations)—adding an element to the end of a list

arithmetic operators—part of most programming languages; for the end of course exam, operators include: addition (+), multiplication (*), subtraction (–), division (/), and modulus (MOD); see order of operations

argument—actual value of parameter being used in a call to a procedure; see "parameter"

ASCII (American Standard Code for Information Interchange)—character encoding scheme used to translate characters into numerical values

assignment operator—allows a program to change a value represented by a variable; in the End-of-Course Exam, the assignment operator is: "←". So a ← 5 means that the variable a is assigned a value of 5.

authentication—digital verification of a person's identity; see Certificate Authorities

authentication cookie—issued by websites and stored on servers, this data is used by web servers to know if a user is logged into a computer or not and the type of account being accessed; see cookie

bandwidth—maximum amount of data that can be sent in a fixed amount of time on a system; analog signals are measured in Hertz (hz) while digital signals are measured in bits per second (bps)

bandwidth throttling—process used by internet service providers to slow service to reduce network traffic

behavior (of a program)—what program does when run; often described by how user interacts with it

bias (in data)—the way in which data was collected does not fairly represent all aspects of what you are trying to measure; cannot be fixed by collecting more data

bias (in design)—the way in which the component (software, algorithm, hardware) was designed does not reflect the way in which all users may need to interface with the component

binary number system—base-2 number system where each place value represents a power of 2 and each digit is 0 or 1

binary search—a search algorithm that finds a target in a sorted set by halving the set being searched at each stage until either the target is found or all elements have been eliminated

bit—a single binary digit, 1 or 0

bitmap graphic—image that is stored as a grid of colored dots; has extension BMP

block-based language—one of two typical languages seen in this course; writing code in this language often involves dragging and dropping blocks of code, rather than typing text; see text-based language

boolean data type—a variable that has a value that is either true or false

boolean logic—branch of algebra where each variable can be either true or false

browser—see web browser

browsing history—list of web page addresses (and related data) that a person has viewed

byte—8 bits (binary digits)

capacity—amount of data that can be stored on a system

Certificate Authorities (CAs)—issue digital certificates that validate ownership of encrypted keys used in secure communications

circuit—one of the hardware components of a computer; a circuit is a complete path that allows electrical current to flow from a high voltage to low voltage

citizen science—collection and analysis of data by non-scientists on home computers; often in collaboration with professional scientists; often to solve scientific problems or perform research

cleaning data—the process of changing data sets so that consistent notations, abbreviations, and spelling was used throughout to make data analysis easier to perform

client/server model (for network)—use of a central computer (server) to manage resources on a network

cloud computing/storage—rather than using a local computer, this form of computation uses a network of remote servers to calculate and/or store data; has fostered new ways to communicate and collaborate

clustering data—grouping data sets together to provide an argument that a pattern exists

code segment—collection of lines of code that make up a program; for text-based code, the collection should be continuous and inside one procedure; for block-based code, the collection should be in the same starter block ("hat" or surrounding block)

code statement—smaller piece of program code that expresses a behavior or action to be performed

collection (as a data type)—type of data that combines elements into one structure; examples: databases, hash tables, dictionaries, sets

color depth—bits per color pixel in an image; example: an 8 bit scheme can create $2^8 = 256$ colors

complexity (of an algorithm)—the amount of logical reasoning required to create an algorithm

computer network—interconnected computing devices that can send or receive data

computing—using computer algorithms to solve problems

computing bias—when a computing system (could be an algorithm, computer, network, or enterprise system) discriminates against individuals or groups of individuals in favor of others

computing device—hardware that can run a program; examples: computer, tablet, server, smart sensor

computing innovation—includes a program as an integral part of its function (can be physical: self-driving car, non-physical software: video editing software, or non-physical concept: social media)

computing system—group of computing devices working together for a common purpose

collaboration—approach to innovating that not only reflects the many ideas of the people in the group that is working together but also avoids bias in the final product because of these perspectives

comments (in a program)—program documentation that is written by programmers to communicate with other programmers; does not impact how program runs

compile error—see syntax error

compression ratio—ratio of the number of bits used to store a file after data compression has been applied to the number of bits used to store a file before data compression has been applied; high ratios like 30:1 indicate more compression so size of file is reduced

condition—a decision in an algorithm (often called a boolean) that is either true or false, used to control selection in an algorithm

confidentiality—keeping a person's information private includes ensuring that the wrong person or system cannot get access to that information

constant—named location that holds data that can be accessed but not changed during program execution

constraint—limit placed to control inputs or outputs

cookie—small amount of data sent from a web server to a browser and stored on a user's computer to remember information about the user's habits like buttons clicked, items in a shopping cart, or commonly filled in fields like name or address; see authentication cookie

correctness (of a program)—depends on correctness of program components, including code segments and procedures

CPU (central processing unit)—the part of a computer that processes instructions; contains the ALU, control unit, and registers

Creative Commons—public copyright license enabling free distribution of work that would otherwise be copyrighted; used to allow creators to share their work for others to use or build upon

credibility—see "source credibility"

crowdsourcing—using the internet to obtain information or input from a large group of people; has led to new models for collaboration such as funding social causes

curated databases—database organized to facilitate research

cryptography—the study of hiding messages or finding hidden messages

cyberattack—attempt to penetrate, use, or access information on another computer or network without permission

cybercrime—criminal activities carried out by using a computer or network

cybersecurity—technology, processes, and practices designed to protect digital data on networks and devices on these networks; includes hardware, software, and human components

cyberwarfare—use of technology by a nation-state to disrupt or damage computers or networks of another nation-state

data abstraction—give a data collection a name without showing all the details of what is represented

database—a large collection of data that can be organized, searched, clustered, classified, transformed, displayed, and/or filtered to gain new insight or to make conclusions

data compression—technique designed to reduce the number of bits stored or transmitted; could be lossy or lossless; see compression ratio

data filtering—the use of a tool to show data that only has certain attributes

data mining—the analysis of large databases to retrieve new information; example of artificial intelligence that has enabled innovation in medicine, business, and science

data stored in list—list data is input through direct initialization list, through computation on list elements, or through computation on other variables

data streaming—transfer of data packets at a high rate to support applications such as high-definition television (HDTV) or music streaming software

data types—what is allowed to be stored in a variable; for example: Booleans, lists, and strings

DDoS (distributed denial-of-service) attack—compromises network device by flooding it with requests from multiple systems

decidable problem —problem in which an algorithm can be constructed to answer 'yes' or 'no' for all inputs

decimal number system—base-10 number system where each place value represents a power of 10 and each digit is 0, 1, 2, 3, 4, 5, 6, 7, 8, or 9

decision problem—problem with a yes/no answer; also called a "decidable problem"

decryption—using mathematical algorithms to decode (decipher) a message; see encryption

design—one of the common phases of the development process, in this phase a developer plans how to accomplish a program specification; may include brainstorming, planning on paper, considering how to break the program into modules, diagramming the user interface and key decisions, deciding on how to test that requirements are being met

desktop computer—personal computer meant to stay in one place

development process—can be exploratory or deliberate, contains the following common phases: investigate/reflect, design, prototype, test; see incremental and iterative development process

digital certificate—forms digital connection between the identity of the recipient and the public key on this certificate; used for authentication step of public key encryption; managed by Certificate Authorities (CAs)

digital data—graphic, sound, text, or numbers represented by discrete digits (like bits)

"digital divide"—expression for the differing access to computing and the internet based on socioeconomic and/or geographic characteristics of a population, group, or person

digital-to-analog converter—device that converts digital data to continuous data

distributed computing—model where multiple devices are used to run a program; allows problems to be solved faster than they could on a single computer; allows problems that could not be solved on one computer due to storage or processing limitations to be solved using more than one computer

distributed system—model where multiple devices communicate and coordinate their actions by passing messages to accomplish a task while appearing to be acting as one system to the user

documentation (of a program)—description of the behavior of a code segment, program, or event and how it was developed

efficiency (of an algorithm)—measure of the computing resources required to execute an algorithm; often represented as a function of the size of the input; formally determined using mathematical reasoning or informally determined by the number of times the algorithm executes for different input sizes

email—message from one computer to one or more recipients via a network; has fostered a new way to communicate and collaborate

effect (of an innovation)—an event that happens as a result of the innovation being used as intended

element (of a list)—one specific item in a list that is assigned a unique index

encryption—using mathematical algorithms to encode (hide) a message so only those that should read it can read it; see symmetric encryption and public key encryption

event (of a program)—associated with an action in a program and supplies input to a program

executable file—file that contains instructions that a computer understands such as how to install software; usually has an .exe extension

exploit—the act of taking advantage of weaknesses (errors or design flaws) in systems to gain access to something that was not intentional in design

expression (in a program)—a code statement that produces a single value; for example: an operator with valid input(s) so a result is produced, a value, a variable, or a call to a procedure that returns a value

fault tolerance—ability of a system to continue functioning even when components in the system fail; the "system" could be a computer, a network, or an enterprise system; redundancy helps to provide this

filtering data—removing parts of data sets to simplify data and/or to make conclusions more evident

firewall—part of a computer system or network that monitors incoming and outgoing communication and decides what will be allowed to travel (in or out) based on security rules

FTP (File Transfer Protocol)—rules for uploading and downloading files from computer to server

freeware—copyrighted software that is given for free by the author or copyright owner

function (of an innovation)—the way in which an innovation works when it is used as intended

functionality (of a program)—how a program behaves when it is executed; often described from perspective of how user interacts with the program

geocoding—use of informal information (see PII) like street addresses to create formal geolocation data

GIF (Graphics Interchange Format)—bitmap graphics file format created for use on the WWW

Gigabyte (GB)—approximately 1 billion bytes; exactly 1,073,741,824 bytes

hardware component—physical part of a computer

heuristic—approach applied to improve an algorithm; may result in approximate solutions instead of exact solutions; may be helpful to find solutions in reasonable time

hierarchical system—system where devices and protocols are in a interdependent relationship and ordered with one central governing body; every member of this system has some other member above it and another member below it with the exception of the central governing body

HTTP (Hypertext Transfer Protocol)—protocol for how web pages are transmitted over the World Wide Web

HTTPS (Hypertext Transfer Protocol Secure)—protocol that creates secure connections by adding an extra layer of encryption; see public key

IDE (Integrated Development Environment)—programming tools combined into one application used to create programs; typically includes editor, debugger, and compiler

IETF (Internet Engineering Task Force)—develop and oversee internet standards and internet protocols

incremental (development process)—breaks a problem into smaller pieces and, only after the smaller piece is tested and working, adds that piece to the whole program

index (of a list)—location in a list, must be greater than 0 or less than or equal to the length of the list in the pseudocode used for the End-of-Course Exam

information (in data)—set of patterns, conclusions, and facts that can be extracted from data

input (to a program)—the data sent to a computer for processing by a program; can be in a variety of forms such as tactile (through touch), audible, visual, or text; an event could be associated with an action and therefore could also supply input data to a program

instance (of a problem)—a specific example of a problem; for example, if the problem is "searching," an instance of that problem is searching for 3 in this list: {4, 5, 3, 2}.

integrated circuit—collection of electronic components such as transistors and resistors that work together to accomplish a goal such as a memory management, motor controller, logic gate, or voltage regulator

intellectual property—invention created and credited to a person or corporation

internet—devices connected to each other via hardware including routers, servers, and other devices, each of which is given an IP address and must follow standardized, open (nonproprietary) protocols

internet, the—the worldwide connection of devices to each other via hardware including routers, servers, and other devices, each of which is given an IP address and must follow protocols

internet standard—evolving "rules" that govern how a device can join and/or communicate on the internet

investigation—one of the common phases of the development process, in this phase the developer is trying to understand and identify program requirements as well as the needs of the user

iteration (in an algorithm)—a loop or repeated behavior in an algorithm; one of three different parts of any algorithm (see sequencing and selection)

IP (Internet Protocol)—one of the protocols used in TCP/IP; responsible for addressing packets so they can be sent to their destination; IPv4 offers 32-bit addresses and IPv6 offers 128-bit addresses

IP addresses—locations (numbers) given to devices connected to a network

iteration (in a program)—a code segment that repeats a specified amount of times or until a given condition is met; recursion is a form of iteration

iterative (development process)—process that uses feedback, testing, and/or reflection throughout the process to support revision and refinement; some changes may require reconsidering earlier changes

key (in encryption or decryption)—number used as an input to an algorithm applied to a block of text to encrypt or decrypt that text; the length of the key is a factor in encryption algorithms

keylogging—use of a program to record the keystrokes made by a user so that sensitive information like passwords can be accessed

kilobyte (KB)—approximately 1,000 bytes; exactly 1,024 bytes

latency—time elapsed between the transmission and receipt of a network request

linear search—a search algorithm that finds a target by looking at each item, one at a time, until the end of the set is reached or the target is found

list—abstract data type that holds an ordered sequence of values (called elements) that can be accessed using index numbers (in the End-of-Course exam, the first index of a list is 1); the use of lists in a program allows related items to be represented using a single variable; lists may be called arrays or arraylists; see "data stored in list" and "using list in program"

logical operator—AND, OR, and NOT; used in program statements to control logical flow of code; compiled when program is run

logic error—see semantic error

lossless data compression—data compression technique where the number of bits needed to store or transmit information is usually reduced and the original data can be reconstructed; typically chosen when the original file needs to be reconstructed or quality matters; example: ZIP, LZ77, RAW, PNG, BMP

lossy data compression—data compression technique where the number of bits needed to store or transmit information is usually reduced, but the original data cannot be reconstructed; this type of compression is preferred when trying to reduce the file size matters more than the ability to reconstruct; example: JPEG image, MP3 audio, MPEG video

MAC address (Media Access Control address)—unique identifier assigned by a manufacturer to equipment that will be ported to a network

machine language—binary code that can be executed by a computer directly

machine learning—study of computer algorithms that improve efficiency and logic through experience; example of artificial intelligence that has enabled innovation in medicine, business, and science

malware—malicious software created to damage or take partial control over a computing system

megabyte (MB)—approximately 1 million bytes; exactly 1,048,276 bytes

memory—computer circuits that hold data that is waiting to be processed

metadata—data about data that provides additional information; if the data is a sound file such as an .mp3, examples of metadata are the song name, the date of the file's creation, or the file size.

mobile computer—any personal computing device not constrained to a desktop

model—a way of representing a real situation in a more abstract way (with less detail)

modularity—breaking a program down into smaller parts often with the use of procedures to manage parts

modulus—operation that returns the remainder of two numbers (for example, the modulus of 7 and 3 is 1)

modem—device that is used to send data from a computer to the internet via phone, cable, or satellite networks

MP3—data compression file format for audio files; example of lossy compression

multifactor authentication—person must provide more than one piece of evidence to prove they are who they say they are; used to control access to a computer or application; usually two of the following: knowledge (something they know), possession (something they have), or inherence (something they are)

non-repudiation—proof that someone cannot deny the validity of their digital signature

open access—online research sources freely available for anyone to use without typical restrictions

open source—programs made freely available to be used or modified by others

operand—the variable on which the operation is to be applied

operator—see arithmetic operator, logical operator, and order of operations

order of operations—the order in which operations are evaluated when more than one operation is used; for arithmetic operators on the End-of-Course exam the order is: (1) parenthesis, (2) exponents, (3) multiply, divide, or modulus, whichever comes first left to right, (4) add or subtract, whichever comes first left to right. In the case of logical operators, the order is: (1) parenthesis, (2) NOT, (3) AND, (4) OR.

optimization problem—problem that might be unsolvable without the use of heuristic; the goal with this type of problem is finding the "best" solution among many; example: traveling salesperson problem

output (from a program)—any data sent from a program to a device, usually based on program's prior state or inputs; can be sent in a variety of forms such as tactile, audible, movement, visual, or text

overflow error—error caused when a program or system receives a number or value that is beyond its defined range of values

packet—way in which data is broken down during data transfer on a network; packets contain data and metadata used to route itself from source to destination

parameter—input variable to a procedure; see argument

parallel computing—computational model where some actions could be performed at the same time as others; takes as long as the time required for any tasks that remain sequential plus the longest of its parallel tasks; solutions that use parallel computing can scale more effectively than those using sequential

parallel processing—use of more than one processor at a time to run a program

path (between two computing devices on a network)—sequence of network connections that occur starting with the sender and ending with the receiver

permission settings—settings that control how your personal information can be accessed and by whom; users should review and maintain these settings to protect their privacy

persistent cookies—cookies that are stored on a local device and remain there after online session ends

personally identifiable information (PII)—information about a person that describes, links, or relates to them; examples: Social Security number, age, race, phone number(s), medical information, biometrics

phishing—cybercrime where an email attempts to obtain personal information from a person

PKI (public key infrastructure)—describes the people, software, hardware, policies, and procedures that are used to manage digital certificates

place value—the worth of a digit in a number. For example: in decimal number 245, the place value of the 2 is 100; in binary number 10, the place value of 1 is 2.

plagiarism—occurs when one person presents another's ideas as their own

problem—description of task that may or may not be solved using an algorithm

procedure—named grouping of programming instructions that may or may not have parameters and return values; used to manage complexity in a program

process—a behavior that uses memory, a central processing unit, input, and/or output that can execute alone or at the same time as other processes

processor—the main controller (or "brain") of a computer; it decides which process(es) will run, for how long, and what inputs to provide and what outputs to receive and share with these processes

program—see "software"

programming language—language used to translate human ideas into software

protocol—set of rules that specify the expected behavior of members of a system

pseudocode—words used to organize thoughts to help you plan how you will write code; pseudocode helps programmers translate specifications (requirements) into code

public key encryption—asymmetric encryption scheme; involves two keys (one private and one public) by pairing a public key for encryption and a private key for decryption where sender does not need receiver's private key to encrypt but the receiver's private key is required to decrypt

purpose (of an innovation or program)—the problem solved or the interest being pursued by the innovator

RAM (Random Access Memory)—memory circuitry that is temporary; holds program instructions, data, and the operating system when the computer is on

reasonable time—way to analyze an algorithm in terms of the number of steps required to solve a problem. An algorithm is said to run in reasonable time if the number of steps the algorithm takes is less than or equal to a polynomial function (constant, linear, square, cube, etc.) of the size of the input.

parameter—input variable of a procedure; see "argument"

procedural abstraction—managing complexity in code by creating a procedure; often that procedure is called more than once

procedure—group of program instructions that may have return values or parameters; procedure may also be referred to as a "method" or "function"

redundancy—the addition of components that will take over the actions of other components if they fail; example: multiple paths of routing data in a network

relational operator—operator that tests a relation between two values; includes: less than ($<$), greater than ($>$), equal to ($=$), not equal to ($\neq$), less than or equal to ($\leq$), and greater than or equal to ($\geq$)

requirements—see "specifications"

rogue access point—the name for a connection on a network that allows data sent over that network to be intercepted, analyzed, and/or modified

ROM (Read Only Memory)—memory circuitry that is permanent and available even after the computer is powered off; used when a computer is turned on so the computer loads what you need to use it

round-off error—error caused when a number exceeds the fixed number of bits allowed in the language

router—device that handles sending data on a network via wired or wireless connection

routing (of packets)—way in which data is sent on a network from sender to receiver

run-time error—mistake in program that happens when program is executed; different languages decide which errors are handled this way

sampling technique—approach used to translate analog data to digital data by measuring values at regular intervals from a source and storing only that sampled data

scalability—ability of a system to change in size to meet new and changing demands

scientific computing—use of advanced computing capabilities to understand and solve complex and often multidisciplinary problems; has enabled innovation in science and business

search engine—a program within a web browser that accepts a search item (query) as an input and uses algorithms to decide and report the best matches to what you searched; can record and maintain history of searches made by users

secure sockets layer/transport layer security (SSL/TLS)—protocols responsible for maintaining secure communications over a network; includes application encryption and character encoding

segments (of a program)—smaller parts of a program

selection (in an algorithm)—the use of a condition to control the logical path taken by an algorithm; one of three different parts of any algorithm (see selection and iteration); includes use of try/exception statements

semantic error—mistake in program that causes it to behave unexpectedly or incorrectly

sensor—device that detects, measures, records, and/or responds to a physical property

sequence (in an algorithm)—the order of the steps of an algorithm matters; one of three different parts of any algorithm (see selection and iteration)

sequential computing—computational model where actions are performed in order, one at a time

server—device that provides data and storage to a network

shareware—copyrighted software that provides users with a trial period to test software and then requires users to pay for it when the time period expires

short-circuit (in boolean logic)—when the result of a logical expression can be evaluated without seeing the entire expression (there are two examples):

(1) TRUE or _____ is always TRUE. It does not matter what comes after the "or".

(2) FALSE and _____ is always FALSE. It does not matter if what is in the blank is TRUE or FALSE.

simulation—a program created to model a real situation with less detail to understand or solve a problem

smart technology—technology that responds to the user and/ or environment; examples: smart grids, smart buildings, smart transportation

SMS (short message service)—short text message, has fostered a new way to collaborate

SMTP (simple mail transfer protocol)— protocol used to send email messages across a network

social engineering—methods used to trick people into sharing PII (personally identifiable information) or engaging in non-secure activities like clicking a link or downloading malicious files

social media—online applications that allow people to share information and connect with others; has fostered a new way to collaborate and communicate

software—collection of program statements that perform a task when run by a computer

solvable problem—a problem that can be solved exactly using an algorithm

source credibility—deciding if a source is reliable based on the reputation and credentials of the author(s), publisher(s), site owner(s), and/or sponsor(s)

specifications—the key details that need to be planned prior to writing an algorithm; examples are the inputs, outputs, data types, and name(s) of procedures called or being created

speed—amount of data per second that can be moved through a system

speedup (of parallel solution)—time it took to complete task sequentially divided by time it took to complete task when handled in parallel; see "parallel computing"

student-developed (procedure/abstraction) code—code that was written by the person who wrote their response to the Create Performance Task

string—ordered sequence of characters

string concatenation—the joining together of two or more strings to make a new string; typically uses a "+" operator

substring—part of a string; for example if str = "HI", "H", and "HI" are substrings. "IH" is not a substring.

SVG (Scalable Vector Graphics)—graphics format for web display that resizes based on screen sizes

symmetric encryption—method of encryption involving one key for encryption and decryption

syntax error—mistake in program caused because rules of the programming language were not followed

targeted advertising—form of advertising that uses data available about a consumer to appeal to that consumer directly

test cases—specific inputs chosen to run through different code segments in a program to check that each code segment works as intended

testing—one of the common phases of the development process, in this phase, a programmer uses planned inputs to verify that the desired outputs/results are occurring

text-based language—one of two types of languages commonly seen in programming; created using a text editor; see "block-based language"

TIFF (tagged image file format)—bitmap image file format that automatically compresses file data; has .tif extension

transistor—one of the building blocks of a circuit, controls flow of electricity by amplifying or redirecting

traversing (a list or array)—using iteration to access each element in a list, one at a time

TCP (Transmission Control Protocol)—protocol within TCP/IP that is responsible for establishing a data connection between devices and managing the breaking down of packets sent across a network; this protocol contains redundancy checks to manage packets that are lost or dropped

trojan—malicious program that appears to perform one function but was created to do something else such as inserting a virus or stealing information like passwords

true color—digital color image with a color depth of 24 or 32 bits

UDP (User Datagram Protocol)—alternative to TCP, responsible for establishing a data connection between two devices and managing the breaking down of packets sent across a network; this protocol does not contain redundancy checks to manage packets that are lost or dropped

URL (Uniform Resource Locator)—the address of a web page; example: http://www.REA.com

undecidable problem—problem that cannot be solved for all instances with a "yes" or "no" answer

using list in program—program creates new data for a list from existing data or the program accesses multiple elements in the list

variable—named location that holds data that can be changed or used during program execution

virus—malicious code that is capable of duplicating itself; often gains access by attaching to legitimate programs and then running independently on a computer

VoIP (Voice over Internet Protocol)—protocols used to make telephone-style calls over the internet

web browser—program on computer that communicates with a web server to display web pages; browsers are governed by protocols set by the Internet Engineering Task Force including hypertext transfer protocol and secure sockets layer/transport layer security.

worm—program designed to enter a system through a vulnerability (called a "hole") then replicate itself and spread to other devices

WWW (World Wide Web)—uses the internet to form system of linked HTTP pages, programs, and files

zero-day attack—malicious attack that exploits previously unknown vulnerabilities in a device, application, or operating system

Helpful Links

Title	Link	Description
ACM Tech News	technews.acm.org	Association for Computing Machinery news page; focused on innovation in computer science, information technology, related science and society
AP® Central	apcentral.collegeboard. org/courses/ap-computer-science-principles	Click "The Exam" tab to find graded samples of student work on the Create Task. Use this to understand how your performance task will be graded.
AP® Classroom	myap.collegeboard.org/ login	After your teacher or Endorsed Provider have passed the Course Audit, they can provide you with access to this site. AP® Classroom contains practice questions to help you prepare for the Create Task and the End-of-Course Exam.
AP® Student Course Page	apstudents.collegeboard. org/courses/ap-computer-science-principles	Provides general information about the course. Under the "About the Exam" tab you will find information about the Create Performance Task (prompts and scoring guidelines) as well as information about how prompts are scored
Credit Policy Search Tool	apstudents.collegeboard. org/getting-credit-placement/ search-policies	Use this tool to find colleges that offer credit or placement for AP® scores
Digital Portfolio	digitalportfolio. collegeboard.org	This is the site you will use to upload your Create Performance Task

Title	Link	Description
Endorsed Course Providers	apcentral.collegeboard.org/courses/ap-computer-science-principles/classroom-resources/curricula-pedagogical-support	This site has a list of course providers who provide training to teachers to learn how to implement AP® CS Principles.
Noodle Tools	noodletools.com	Online tool to help you with the creation of citations. Use this to cite any images or code used for the Create Task that you did not create.
NPR Technology	npr.org/sections/technology	Source for technology-related news articles and stories.
Online Course Providers	apstudents.collegeboard.org/courses/ap-computer-science-principles/online-course-providers	This site has a list of course providers that are available to you if you are taking this course independently.
Science Daily	sciencedaily.com/news/computers_math	Articles related to innovations in computer science; can filter for articles focused on distributed computing, parallel processing, algorithms, etc.
Wikimedia Commons	commons.wikimedia.org/wiki	This site has digital files (images, sounds, and videos) shared by authors who provide permission for you to use them, including information about how to cite.

Create Performance Task Submission Requirements

These requirements can be accessed directly on the following site: *apcentral. collegeboard.org/pdf/ap-csp-student-task-directions.pdf*. When you are ready to hand in your responses, you will copy and paste each response and submit via the Digital Portfolio.

1. PROGRAM CODE (can be created *independently or collaboratively*)

   Submit one PDF file that contains all of your program code (including comments). Include comments or acknowledgments for any part of the submitted program code that has been written by someone other than you and/or your collaborative partner(s).

   IMPORTANT: *If the programming environment allows you to include comments, this is the preferred way to acknowledge and give credit to another author. However, if the programming environment does not allow you to include comments, you can add them in a document editor when you capture your program code for submission.*

   In your program, you must include student-developed program code that contains the following:

> **DEFINITION:**
>
> **List**
>
> A list is an ordered sequence of elements. The use of the lists allows multiple related items to be represented using a single variable. Lists may be referred to by different names such as arrays depending on the programming language.
>
> **DEFINITION:**
>
> **Collection Type**
>
> A collection type is a type that aggregates elements in a single structure. Some examples include lists, databases, hash tables, dictionaries, and sets.
>
> **IMPORTANT:**
>
> With text-based program code you can use the print command to save your program code as a PDF file, or you can copy and paste your code to a text document and then convert it into a PDF file.
>
> With block-based program code, you can create screen captures that include only your program code, paste these images into a document, and then convert that document to a PDF. Sreen captures should not be blurry and text should be at least 10 pt font size.
>
> Source: *AP® Computer Science Principles Course and Exam Description (2020)*, The College Board

> ▸ Instructions for input from one of the following:
>
>   - the user (including user actions that trigger events)
>
>   - a device
>
>   - an online data stream
>
>   - a file
>
> ▸ Use of at least one **list** (or other **collection type**) to represent a collection of data that is stored and used to manage program complexity and help fulfill the program's purpose

IMPORTANT: The data abstraction must make the program easier to develop (alternatives would be more complex) or easier to maintain (future changes to the size of the list would otherwise require significant modifications to the program code).

> ▸ At least one procedure that contributes to the program's intended purpose, where you have defined:
>
>   - the procedure's name
>
>   - the return type (if necessary)
>
>   - one or more parameters

IMPORTANT: Implementation of built-in or existing procedures or language structures, such as event handlers or main methods, are not considered student-developed.

> - An algorithm that includes sequencing, selection, and iteration that is in the body of the selected procedure
>
> - Calls to your student-developed procedure
>
> - Instructions for output (tactile, audible, visual, or textual) based on input and program functionality

2. VIDEO (created <u>independently</u>)

   Submit one video file that demonstrates the running of your program as described below. Collaboration is **not** allowed during the development of your video.

   Your video must demonstrate your program running, including:

   - Input to your program

- At least one aspect of the functionality of your program
- Output produced by your program

Your video may NOT contain:

- Any distinguishing information about yourself
- Voice narration (though text captions are encouraged)

Your video must be:

- Either .mp4, .wmv, .avi, or .mov format
- No more than 1 minute in length
- No more than 30MB in file size

3. WRITTEN RESPONSES (created independently)

Submit your responses to prompts 3a—3d, which are described below. Your response to all prompts combined must not exceed 750 words (program code is not included in the word count). Collaboration is **not** allowed on the written responses. Instructions for submitting your written responses are available on the AP® Computer Science Principles Exam Page on AP® Central. The link to this page is here: *apcentral.collegeboard.org/courses/ap-computer-science-principles/exam.*

3a. Provide a written response that does all three of the following:

Approx. 150 words (for all subparts of 3a combined)

i. Describes the overall purpose of the program

ii. Describes what functionality of the program is demonstrated in the video

iii. Describes the input and output of the program demonstrated in the video

---

DEFINITION:

List

A list is an ordered sequence of elements. The use of the lists allows multiple related items to be represented using a single variable. Lists may be referred to by different names such as arrays depending on the programming language.

DEFINITION:

Collection Type

A collection type is a type that aggregates elements in a single structure. Some examples include lists, databases, hash tables, dictionaries, and sets.

IMPORTANT:

The data abstraction must make the program easier to develop (alternatives would be more complex) or easier to maintain (future changes to the size of the list would otherwise require significant modifications to the program code).

IMPORTANT:

Built-in or existing procedures and language structures, such as event handlers and main methods, are not considered student-developed

Source: *AP® Computer Science Principles Course and Exam Description (2020)*, The College Board.

3b. Capture and paste two program code segments you developed during the administration of this task that contain a list (or other collection type) being used to manage complexity in your program.

Approx. 200 words (for all subparts of 3b combined, exclusive of program code)

i. The first program code segment must show how data have been stored in the list.

ii. The second program code segment must show the data in the same list being used, such as creating new data from the existing data or accessing multiple elements in the list, as part of fulfilling the program's purpose.

Then, provide a written response that does all three of the following:

iii. Identifies the name of the list being used in this response

iv. Describes what the data contained in the list represent in your program

v. Explains how the selected list manages complexity in your program code by explaining why your program code could not be written, or how it would be written differently, if you did not use the list

3c. Capture and paste two program code segments you developed during the administration of this task that contain a student-developed procedure that implements an algorithm used in your program and a call to that procedure.

Approx. 200 words (for all subparts of 3c combined, exclusive of program code)

i. The first program code segment must be a student-developed procedure that:

- Defines the procedure's name and return type (if necessary)

- Contains and uses one or more parameters that have an effect on the functionality of the procedure

- Implements an algorithm that includes sequencing, selection, and iteration

   ii.   The second program code segment must show where your student-developed procedure is being called in your program.

Then, provide a written response that does both of the following:

   iii.   Describes in general what the identified procedure does and how it contributes to the overall functionality of the program

   iv.   Explains in detailed steps how the algorithm implemented in the identified procedure works. Your explanation must be detailed enough for someone else to recreate it.

3d. Provide a written response that does all three of the following:

Approx. 200 words (for all subparts of 3d combined)

   i.   Describes two calls to the procedure identified in written response 3c. Each call must pass a different argument(s) that causes a different segment of code in the algorithm to execute.

First call:

Second call:

   ii.   Describes what condition(s) is being tested by each call to the procedure

Condition(s) tested by the first call:

Condition(s) tested by the second call:

   iii.   Identifies the result of each call

Result of the first call:

Result of the second call:

Create Performance Task Scoring Checklist

This table is a summary of the Create Performance Task guidelines. The full scoring guidelines are available here: *apcentral.collegeboard.org/pdf/ap-computer-science-principles-2021-create-performance-task-scoring-guidelines.pdf*

Reporting Category	Connection to Create PT	What you need to do to maximize your score for each category:
Program Purpose and Function	Video and Prompt 3a	• Video demonstrates running of program including input, program functionality, and output AND Prompt 3a needs to describe: • purpose of program • the functionality of the program from the video • the input of the program from the video • the output of the program from the video

Reporting Category	Connection to Create PT	What you need to do to maximize your score for each category:
2	Prompt 3b (i–iv)	Within Prompt 3b, parts i–iv, you need to: • include two program code segments to: (1) show how data has been stored in the list (or other collection type) and (2) show the data in the same list being used as a part of fulfilling purpose of program • identify the name of the variable representing the list • describe what the data in the list represents for the program
3	Prompt 3b (v)	Within Prompt 3b, part v, you need to: • refer to the same program code segments shared in parts i and ii • within these code segments, show a list being used to manage complexity in the program • explain how this selected list manages complexity by either (1) explaining why the program could not be written without this list or (2) how the program would be written differently without this list
4	Prompt 3c (i–iii)	Within Prompt 3c, parts i–iii, you need to: • include two program code segments to: (1) show a procedure you developed independently with at least one parameter that has an effect on the functionality of the procedure and (2) show where this procedure is being called • describe what this procedure does and how it contributes to the overall functionality of the program

Reporting Category	Connection to Create PT	What you need to do to maximize your score for each category:
5	Prompt 3c (iv)	Within Prompt 3c, part iv, you need to: • refer to the same program code segments shared in parts i and ii • within these code segments, you need to have an algorithm that you created that shows sequencing, selection, and iteration • explain how the algorithm you created works in steps that are detailed enough that someone else could recreate the algorithm from your writing
6	Prompt 3c Procedure, Prompt 3d (i-iii)	Within Prompt 3d, parts i–iii, you need to: • refer to the procedure you wrote about in Prompt 3c • describe two calls to this procedure—each call needs to pass a different argument that causes a different code segment in the algorithm to execute • describe the condition(s) being tested by each call to the procedure • identify the result of each call to the procedure

Exam Reference Sheet

Instruction	Explanation
Assignment	
Text: a ← expression Block: a ← expression	Evaluates expression and then assigns the result to the variable a.
Text: DISPLAY(expression) Block: DISPLAY expression	Displays the value of expression, followed by a space.
Text: INPUT () Block: INPUT	Accepts a value from the user and returns the input value.
Arithmetic Operators and Numeric Procedures	
Text and Block: a + b a − b a * b a / b	The arithmetic operators +, −, *, and / are used to perform arithmetic on a and b. For example, 17/5 evaluates to 3.4.

(continued)

Instruction	Explanation
Arithmetic Operators and Numeric Procedures (continued)	
Text and Block: a MOD b	Evaluates to the remainder when a is divided by b. Assume that a is an integer greater than or equal to 0 and b is an integer greater than 0. For example, 17 MOD 5 evaluates to 2. The order of operations used in mathematics applies when evaluating expressions.
Text: RANDOM a,b Block: RANDOM $\boxed{a,b}$	Generates and returns a random integer from a to b, including a and b. Each result is equally likely to occur. For example, RANDOM (1, 3) could evaluate 1, 2, or 3.
Relational and Boolean Operators	
Text and Block: a = b a ≠ b a > b a < b a ≥ b a ≤ b	The relational operators =, ≠, >, <, ≥, and ≤ are used to test the relationship between two variables, expressions, or values. A comparison using relational operators evaluates to a Boolean value. For example, a = b evaluates to true if a and b are equal; otherwise, it evaluates to false.

Instruction	Explanation
Relational and Boolean Operators (continued)	
Text: `NOT condition` Block: `NOT`(`condition`)	Evaluates to `true` if condition is `false`; otherwise evaluates to `false`.
Text: `condition1 AND condition2` Block: (`condition1`)`AND`(`condition2`)	Evaluates to `true` if both `condition1` and `condition2` are `true`; otherwise evaluates to `false`.
Text: `condition1 OR condition2` Block: (`condition1`)`OR`(`condition2`)	Evaluates to `true` if `condition1` is `true` or if `condition2` is `true` or if both `condition1` and `condition2` are `true`; otherwise evaluates to `false`.
Selection	

Text:
`IF (condition)`
`{`
   `<block of statements>`
`}`
Block:
`IF`(`condition`)
(`block of statements`)
	The code in `block of statements` is executed if the Boolean expression condition evaluates to `true`; no action is taken if condition evaluates to `false`.

Instruction	Explanation
Selection (continued)	

Text:
 	
IF (condition)
{
   `<first block of statements>`
}
ELSE
{
   `<second block of statements>`
}
Block:
 	
	The code in first block of statements is executed if the Boolean expression condition evaluates to true; otherwise, the code in second block of statements is executed.

Instruction	Explanation
Iteration	

Text:
 	
REPEAT n TIMES
{
   `<block of statements>`
}
 	
Block:
 	
REPEAT n TIMES
 	
   block of statements
	The code in `block of statements` is executed n times.

Text:
 	
REPEAT UNTIL (condition)
{
   `<block of statements>`
}
 	
Block:
 	
REPEAT UNTIL condition
 	
   block of statements
	The code in `block of statements` is repeated until the Boolean expression `condition` evaluates to true.

List Operations	
For all list operations, if a list index is less than 1 or greater than the length of the list, an error message is produced and the program terminates.	
Text: aList ← [value1, value2, value3, ...] Block: aList ← value1, value2, value3	Creates a new list that contains the values value1, value2, value3, and ... at indices 1, 2, 3, and ..., respectively and assigns it to aList.

Instruction	Explanation
List Operations (continued)	
Text: aList ← [ ] Block: (aList ←☐)	Creates an empty list and assigns it to aList.
Text: aList ← bList Block: (aList ← bList)	Assigns a copy of the list bList to the list aList. For example, if bList contains [20, 40, 60], then aList will also contain [20, 40, 60] after the assignment.
Text: aList[i] Block: aList $\boxed{i}$	Accesses the element of aList at index i. The first element of aList is at index 1 and is accessed using the notation aList[1].
Text: x ← aList[i] Block: (x ← aList $\boxed{i}$)	Assigns the value of aList[i] to the variable x.
Text: aList[i] ← x Block: (aList $\boxed{i}$ ← x)	Assigns the value of x to aList[i].
Text: x ← aList[i] Block: (aList $\boxed{i}$ ← aList $\boxed{j}$)	Assigns the value of aList[i] to aList[j].

Instruction	Explanation
List Operations (continued)	

Text:
`INSERT (aList, i, value)`
Block:
`( INSERT [aList, i, value] )`
	Any values in aList at indices greater than or equal to i are shifted to the right. The length of list is increased by 1, and value is placed at index i in aList.

Text:
`APPEND (aList, value)`
Block:
`( APPEND [aList, value] )`
	The length of aList is increased by 1, and value is placed at the end of aList.

Text:
`REMOVE (aList, i)`
Block:
`( REMOVE [aList, i] )`
	Removes the item at index i in aList and shifts to the left any values at indices greater than i. The length of aList is decreased by 1.

Text:
`LENGTH (aList)`
Block:
`LENGTH [aList]`
	Evaluates to the number of elements in aList.

Text:
`FOR EACH item IN aList`
`{`
`    <block of statements>`
`}`
Block:
`( FOR EACH item IN aList`
`  ( block of statements ) )`
	The variable item is assigned the value of each element of aList sequentially, in order, from the first element to the last element. The code in block of statements is executed once for each assignment of item.

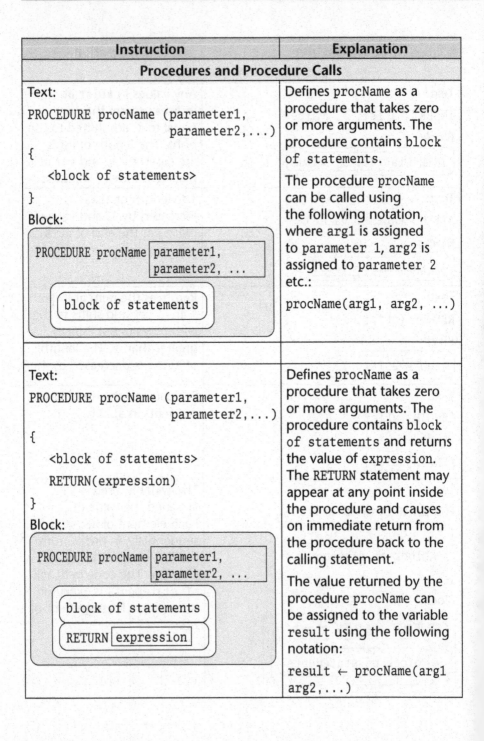

Instruction	Explanation
Procedures and Procedure Calls	

Text:
 	
PROCEDURE procName (parameter1,
                    parameter2,...)
{
 	
  <block of statements>
 	
}
Block:
 	
PROCEDURE procName | parameter1,
                     parameter2, ...
 	
  block of statements
	Defines procName as a procedure that takes zero or more arguments. The procedure contains block of statements.
	
	The procedure procName can be called using the following notation, where arg1 is assigned to parameter 1, arg2 is assigned to parameter 2 etc.:
	
	procName(arg1, arg2, ...)

Text:
 	
PROCEDURE procName (parameter1,
                    parameter2,...)
{
 	
  <block of statements>
  RETURN(expression)
 	
}
Block:
 	
PROCEDURE procName | parameter1,
                     parameter2, ...
 	
  block of statements
 	
  RETURN | expression
	Defines procName as a procedure that takes zero or more arguments. The procedure contains block of statements and returns the value of expression. The RETURN statement may appear at any point inside the procedure and causes on immediate return from the procedure back to the calling statement.
	
	The value returned by the procedure procName can be assigned to the variable result using the following notation:
	
	result ← procName(arg1 arg2,...)

Instruction	Explanation
Procedures and Procedure Calls (continued)	
Text: RETURN(expression) Block: (RETURN [expression])	Returns the flow of control to the point where the procedure was called and returns the value of expression.
Robot	
If the robot attempts to move to a square that is not open or is beyond the edge of the grid, the robot will stay in its current location and the program will terminate.	
Text: MOVE_FORWARD () Block: (MOVE_FORWARD)	The robot moves one square forward in the direction it is facing.
Text: ROTATE_LEFT () Block: (ROTATE_LEFT)	The robot rotates in place 90 degrees counterclockwise (i.e., makes an in-place left turn).
Text: ROTATE_RIGHT () Block: (ROTATE_RIGHT)	The robot rotates in place 90 degrees clockwise (i.e., makes an in-place right turn).
Text: CAN_MOVE (direction) Block: CAN_MOVE [direction]	Evaluates to true if there is an open square one square in the direction relative to where the robot is facing; otherwise evaluates to false. The value of direction can be left, right, forward, or backward.

Source: AP® Computer Science Principles Course and Exam Description (2020), The College Board

Notes